The Ends of the Earth

The Ends of the Earth

Morris Panych

Talonbooks   Vancouver   1993

Copyright © 1993 Morris Panych

Published with the assistance of the Canada Council

Talonbooks
201 - 1019 East Cordova
Vancouver, British Columbia
Canada V6A 1M8

Typeset in Palatino by Pièce de Résistance Ltée., and printed and bound in Canada by Hignell Printing Ltd.

First Printing: October 1993

Canadian Cataloguing in Publication Data

    Panych, Morris, 1952 -
      The Ends of the Earth

      A play.
      ISBN 0-88922-334-3

      I. Title.
      PS8581.A65E5 1993   C812'.54   C93-091738-3
      PR9199.3.P36E5 1993

The Ends of the Earth was first produced at the Arts Club
Theatre in Vancouver, in September 1992, with the
following cast:

FRANK	Alec Willows
WALKER	Earl Pastko
WILLY	Wendy Gorling
ALICE	Patti Allan
FINN	Tom McBeath

Directed by Morris Panych
Set Design by Ken MacDonald
Costume Design by Nancy Tait
Lighting Design by Marsha Sibthorpe
Stage Manager: Marion Anderson

It subsequently played at Toronto's Tarragon Theatre later
the same year, with this cast:

FRANK	Stephen Ouimette
WALKER	Keith Knight
WILLY	Wendy Thatcher
ALICE	Ellen-Ray Hennessy
FINN	John Dolan

Directed by Morris Panych
Set and Costume Design by Ken MacDonald
Lighting Design by Paul Mathiesen
Stage Manager: Tony Ambrosi

The Characters

In order of appearance:

WILLY, a woman with conceptual problems
ALICE, her blind companion
CLAYTON, a police detective
FRANK, a man of about forty
HENRY WALKER, another man, about the same age
ASTRID, a woman who was FRANK's lover
FINN, Editor of *The Free Advertiser Weekly*, and FRANK's
  boss
HOMEOWNER
LIBBY, REGGIE, MAG, apartment dwellers on an
         intercom
JACK, friendly old neighbour of Mr. Walker's
JUNE, a bus depot waitress
LAWRENCE, a professional truck driver
MONA, an actress and wanderer
MILLIE, a gifted psychic
SERGIO, a friend of MILLIE's
LEWIS, a travel agent
EDUARDO, a Spanish sailor
FERRYMAN

Suggested breakdown of parts:

ACTOR 1: Frank
ACTOR 2: Henry Walker, Reggie
ACTOR 3: Willy, Libby, Astrid, Millie
ACTOR 4: Alice, June, Mag, Mona
ACTOR 5: Finn, Homeowner, Clayton, Jack, Lawrence,
     Sergio, Eduardo, Lewis, Ferryman

Act One

The play takes place in many "locations," sometimes moving from place to place in only a moment. In a way we never really know where we are, except perhaps through the action.

The character of CLAYTON is often out of time. He appears, sometimes unexpectedly, at times speaking his lines as he appears, at others speaking before he is seen.

In the first scene, WILLY, a slightly confused older woman, gazes out at the world from a verandah somewhere, the wind blowing her hair. ALICE is unravelling an old sweater, as WILLY takes up the yarn. ALICE suddenly stops.

WILLY
It's nothing, Alice.

ALICE
Someone's coming up the road.

WILLY
A gentleman.

ALICE

Tell him to go away, Willy. God knows — this hotel is no place for visitors. *(Taking the wool, she disappears)*

CLAYTON

(Approaching, a little out of breath) Hello, ma'am. Mind if I ask you a few questions?

WILLY

You're not with the management, I take it.

CLAYTON

Ma'am?

WILLY

I suppose you'd like to see a room?

CLAYTON

I'd like to see them all.

WILLY goes, and CLAYTON follows, closing a door behind him. The wind picks up.

Music. Lights fade. Music up full. Credits.

FRANK, a man of about forty sits alone in a chair, beneath a bare light bulb; CLAYTON stands to one side.

CLAYTON

So?

FRANK

So?

CLAYTON

(Coming up close and standing over him) So why'd you do it, Frank?

FRANK

Do what?

CLAYTON

Let's start from the beginning.

FRANK

(As he speaks, a transition) I don't know how I managed to get involved in this. Who am I? My importance could be measured in grams. If you measured the weight of these things. Imagine if people actually weighed what they were worth, I've often thought.

CLAYTON

Have you.

FRANK

The point is, I'd be a lot thinner than I am. The point is, I'm no one at all, really. My father was a high school teacher. Did I mention that? Physics. It's where I get my sense of humour. My mother, what was left of her, died a few years ago, of something. Left the linen neatly folded.

CLAYTON

Is this actually going anywhere, Frank?

FRANK

(FRANK is slowly joined by a group of people) I do hope so, Clayton. After all, it's my life we're talking about here. And a person always likes to imagine their life as going somewhere. As having — shape — perhaps — a kind of narrative — even though it might not seem that way when you're living it. In my case, there is nothing extraordinarily — novel — to report about me, or anybody I know. A neighbour of mine won a door prize, once, somewhere. Money was involved, but I don't know how much. It wasn't millions, although you would have

9

thought as much. Most people I know are exceedingly surprised if anything at all happens. They get on with their lives and that's pretty much it. Open the door to get a newspaper and close it again. Oh sure, there was a time when things happened. Out in the open air. In the park. On a city street. When life expressed itself with more — absolute certainty. When conversations flowed like — ginger ale into a glass. When there was music playing somewhere — at night. But, now it's pretty much — nothing at all. The flickering of television light from some window. A cat — off doing something. A garbage can lid going — clunk. People are more private about things. Live lives that are intentionally dull. And who can blame them? There's a kind of insane anger on the loose everywhere. Is it any wonder people avoid things? Move in crowds? The less you're noticed, the better off you are. Obscurity. It's what's made this country so...well — not great but certainly — prudent. Unheroic. I admire the weakness of the national character. One can so easily conform to it. Personally, I like travelling in the company of others. I...I feel...felt...safe in a group. It was one of my philosophies in life. Never go off on your own. Never get separated from the rest.

As FRANK remains in place, the group goes off in a clump.

So, you see, I can't understand *how* I ever allowed myself to stand out the way I did. But there I was. I had always tried to act like I wasn't there, but the truth is, there's just no getting around your own existence.

The group is gone, except for one man, WALKER, standing alone.

It follows you everywhere. The throbbing toothache. The irritating little flea bite on the ankle. The — the — leg that falls asleep, forcing you to drag yourself up the aisle of some movie theatre. The tickle in the throat, accompanied by the embarrassing and pathetic little — *(Coughs)* cough. The point is — you don't want to draw anyone's attention, and the point is — I did.

WALKER looks suspiciously towards FRANK.

Towards me. This gentleman who otherwise might never have noticed me. You see — I was sitting there, just — quietly, mindlessly, thinking of — sheer space — and into that space there sprouted this *thought* — *this thought* — about acting on impulse, doing whatever occurs to you — on the spur of the moment — something like that. I'm sure you know what I'm talking about — it's that — thought you shouldn't have — but do — of leaping off a bridge as you cross it, or shouting something perfectly obscene at the top of your lungs during some Sunday afternoon chamber concert. Yes. And almost without realizing it, the way you hardly ever realize what you're doing until it's done, I found myself — at this bus stop — sort of — folding my tongue in half, like this. *(FRANK does a contortion with his tongue, turning, in mid-action, towards WALKER)* It wasn't just that he noticed me. He took out a little note-pad and jotted something down. And then he left.

WALKER leaves abruptly.

Abruptly.

The scene changes to a park.

ASTRID

So?

FRANK

Astrid and I. Wandering through the park. I think it's
autumn. Not that she'd have noticed. Astrid was
completely oblivious to the world around her. In a way, I
envied that. Whenever we ate in restaurants, those
restaurants, you know those ones, on the very edge of
civilization, she always managed to seat herself with her
back to the frothing maniac, in the wool hat, making odd
stabbing gestures at me with his steak knife. Or the old
woman in the green plastic bag. I'd say to Astrid, "Let's
get out of here, before we're murdered, shall we."

ASTRID & FRANK

It's just another lunatic.

FRANK

She'd say. As if that would somehow make them all
disappear into thin air. *(To ASTRID)* But *he* wasn't like
that. *He* was different. It was his ordinariness that was so
exceptional. His complete lack of any distinguishing
characteristics. Except, of course, for the notepad. Are you
listening to me by any chance? *(To audience again)* She
never listened to me. Always looked right past me. It was
as if someone more interesting might come along at any
minute. Eventually someone did. *(To ASTRID)* Astrid,
this is serious. I think someone is following me.

ASTRID

Where?

FRANK

What do you mean, "where"? Following me. Last night he
was there again. Same corner. With the notebook. This
morning. He's on the bus. Pretending he's going
someplace. The whole time furtively glancing back at me.
Making another entry. Oh my God, don't look now —
there's a woman with a saucepan on her head. Over there.

By those trees. What's going on in the world? I stick my tongue out for a second and people start secret files on me, and yet some woman can wander around in a public park wearing an aluminum pot for a hat and nobody thinks twice. It isn't fair.

                    ASTRID
What isn't?

                    FRANK
Never mind. *(To audience)* Astrid was depressed again.

                    ASTRID
Who are you talking to?

                    FRANK
The world, Astrid. Just in case somebody's listening. What are you dreaming about, Astrid?

                    ASTRID
Huh?

                    FRANK
Obviously I'm being investigated. Doesn't that concern you in any way? My life is under serious scrutiny here.

                    ASTRID
I don't really love you anymore, Frank.

                    FRANK
God knows who's behind all — this.

   Pause.

I see. Did you *ever* love me?

                    ASTRID
No.

FRANK

Oh.

ASTRID

But you cheered me up a little.

FRANK

So? Is there anything wrong with that?

ASTRID

I don't think I was meant to be happy. *(She wanders off)*

FRANK

(Calling) I was! *(By himself)* I don't believe this. I'd
cheered her up a little. Apparently too little. Off she went
with some guy in a beret. A beret. *(Despairing)* Does
anybody really love anybody anymore? I should have
known. She used to answer the phone when we were in
the middle of having sex. Just in case, I suppose. That's the
thing about phones, I always say. Unlike people, they have
to be answered.

The phone rings in his apartment and we are there.

There. You see how it demands your immediate attention.
(A pause while it rings) For all I know it could be him. Or
someone who works for him. He'd know my phone
number by now. Wouldn't he? Yesterday he followed me,
as far as the corner. When I turned around suddenly, he
ducked into a hardware store. Right, I thought. Very
clever. I went back and I watched him through the
window. Pretending to be interested. In hardware. He
bought a pair of wire strippers. I ask you. What does any
ordinary man in the twentieth century want with a pair of
wire strippers? I ducked into the alley when he came out.
And waited for a minute until he passed. Then I followed
him a couple of blocks until he turned into his building.

And where do you suppose *that* was? I'll tell you where.
The apartment building directly across from where I lived!
That's where! *(Music)* As I watched him go, I wondered.
How much of my life would he strip away before it was
completely gone?

FINN
(In an office of the newspaper) Call the police.

FRANK
You think I haven't thought of them? I've thought of
everything. I can't stop thinking. He's too smart for the
police. He hasn't done anything yet. Nothing you or I
would notice anyway. But then again, who knows with
these people.

FINN
What people?

FRANK
Exactly.

FINN
If he's harassing you....

FRANK
Are you listening to me? He isn't *doing* anything. He's just
there. All the time. Everywhere I go.

FINN
Do you have any real estate? He might be wanting to sell
it for you.

FRANK
(More to himself) For all I know he could be *with* the police.
(To FINN) What? I haven't got anything anybody wants.

FINN
Maybe he wants to save your soul.

FRANK
With a pair of wire strippers?

FINN
It could be something you wrote.

FRANK
In a gardening column? Who could possibly be offended?
A weed?

FINN
Listen.

FRANK
Come to think of it, I did a real hatchet piece on aphids a
while back.

FINN
Maybe he's an animal rights activist.

FRANK
He could have twisted things around in his own mind.
People do that, you know.

FINN
Print a retraction.

FRANK
Mr. Finn — I have my credibility. As a newspaper man.

FINN
You do?

FRANK
Mr. Finn was the publisher of a paper to which I was a

regular contributor. It was called *The Free Advertiser Weekly*. I was also the circulation manager. And the typesetter. As well I sold the advertising. In fact I was the head of advertising. In fact I was the head of everything. *(On the street now)* Which meant I was also the head of distribution, which meant I delivered the paper. Door to door.

                    HOMEOWNER
(Calling from off) I don't want this.

                    FRANK
It's free.

                    HOMEOWNER
I don't care. I don't want it.

   The paper is thrown FRANK's way.

                    FRANK
How can you not want it?! It's *free*, you idiot! What could be more desirable than a free thing?! The whole *concept* here is that you want it because it doesn't cost anything. Or have you missed the entire point of this, you great, pompous — tit! *(By himself)* Good God. What's happening to me? I've never lost control like that before. It's the stress of this — this — the pressure of this — *thing* following me — this — but *really*, it's just hard to believe that a free newspaper could have circulation problems. I suppose people are overloaded with information now. And you begin to discover that life is like a big rock. You don't necessarily want to turn it over and see what's underneath. Unless you're an entomologist, that is. Did I mention that I studied insects once? In college. In seemed like the natural field for me. There are a few exceptions, of course, but generally I like insects. If nothing else for their

sheer numbers. With insects, there's always a crowd. But I gave up the study when I realized that most people in the field of entomology seemed to end up in the extermination business. It felt rather self-defeating. So I began to write poetry on the subject, which proved vastly unpopular but did give me a feeling for literary composition. I turned to writing fiction next. But that never really worked out. My style is rather — lifeless. I can't even tell a joke, without everybody becoming — sort of — concerned. So I began writing about gardens. I can't imagine there being anything so perfect as those. To look at a garden you wouldn't know what's really going on. So much quiet dignity concealing so much seething underground insect activity. And after all, my name is Gardener. Well, what else would it be? For so long I *tried* to avoid becoming one. If I didn't know better I'd say my whole life had been plotted out for me, like carrot seeds. In neat little rows. "Say. Whatever happened to Frank *Gardener*?" "Gosh, I wonder." There I was. At *The Free Advertiser Weekly*. A gardening columnist. It wasn't much, but I suppose it was something.

FINN
(*Back at the newspaper*) By the way, I'm phasing out the features.

FRANK
What? There'll be nothing but advertising. What kind of newspaper is that?

FINN
A successful one.

FRANK
When I started here, this was sort of a left-wing newspaper. Wasn't it?

                         FINN
Things change, Frank.

                         FRANK
By the way, I'm calling myself Miles now.

                         FINN
Miles?

                         FRANK
Travers. I feel I need an alias.

                         FINN
Why?

                         FRANK
Why else?

                         FINN
What? This guy? He's still following you?

                         FRANK
I need to find out what's going on here.

                         FINN
Why don't you take some time off, then?

                         FRANK
What? Here? I'm indispensable here.

                         FINN
Frank, listen.

                         FRANK
Miles.

FINN

Whatever. Listen. I wish I could say you've been like a son to me, but you haven't. I never had a son. I'm impotent.

FRANK

I didn't know that.

FINN

Everyone else does.

FRANK

They do?

FINN

So, I have nobody to leave the paper to.

FRANK

That's a dangling preposition.

FINN

It sure the hell is. What? Listen. Eventually — I'll sell the paper. Retire and go someplace. The wife and I only have a few years left, so I'd like to get away from her as much as I possibly can now.

FRANK

I can't imagine you selling this. You put your whole life into this, Mr. Finn.

FINN

Not really.

FRANK

I could run this paper. (I'm running it now).

FINN

You want to end up like me? Hell. My life was over before it even started. You don't want to stay here, Frank. *(Going)* There's no future in this.

FRANK

(Calling) Miles! *(Alone now)* I don't *want* a future. I just want to be part of something. Anything. Even if it is *The Free Advertiser Weekly.* Was.

Instantly applying a false moustache, as the scene returns to a park.

I'm not interested in being singled out in any way. Identified.

ASTRID

So where is he, then?

FRANK

Well, you can't *see* him, Astrid. He operates with a certain degree of professionalism. Don't trivialize the situation.

ASTRID

Is that a real moustache, Frank?

FRANK

(Quietly) Please. I'm calling myself Miles now. Miles Travers.

ASTRID

You are?

FRANK

Who knows? Maybe a change of name will bring a change of...luck. I've checked into a hotel. For the time being.

A look from ASTRID.

I can't tell you which one.

> ASTRID

I wasn't asking.

> FRANK

Necessary precaution. *(Pause)* Sorry. I thought you were asking.

> ASTRID

I wasn't.

> FRANK

I'm glad none of this is causing you any undue concern.

> ASTRID

I'm moving in with him, Frank.

> FRANK

Miles.

> ASTRID

Miles.

> FRANK

You're moving in with him. Do I need to know this?

> ASTRID

We thought maybe we'd have a child.

> FRANK

A child?

> ASTRID

I don't know.

FRANK
You're having a child with a man who wears a beret?

ASTRID
Beret? He's a lawyer. You're thinking of that other guy.

FRANK
I am? Yes I am. And what happened to *him*?

ASTRID
I didn't really love him.

FRANK
Do you really love the *lawyer*.

ASTRID
No. But he's trying to talk me into it. *(She drifts off in a sad dream)*

FRANK
I see. *(Calling after her)* So he's actually a *solicitor* then.

ASTRID's gone.

And the rest of us were like the trees in Astrid's sad forest. Felled one by one, to clear her a winding path. Don't get me wrong. I didn't mind being part of someone's trail-blazing history. A mere statistic is not a bad thing to have been, I suppose. Preferable to being *noted* in life.

FRANK goes off, and WALKER appears from the opposite way, making a note.

WALKER
Left — the — park. Going — west.

CLAYTON

(Appearing) Did you follow him?

WALKER

Yes.

CLAYTON

And?

WALKER

(With meaning) He checked into a hotel.

CLAYTON

That's not unusual.

WALKER

No. Not if you're from out of town.

They give each other a look, then go off in opposite directions.

The scene changes to an apartment building entrance, as FRANK speaks to residents through the intercom.

FRANK

What is it about intercoms?

LIBBY

I don't know what you're talking about. There's no one here by that name.

FRANK

(Speaking through the intercom) What name? I didn't give you a name.

LIBBY

(Through the intercom) Yes you did.

FRANK

No, I didn't. Hello. Hello.

LIBBY

Go away.

FRANK

Hello? How could she not trust me? She didn't even know me. Ma'am? *(Tries buzzing another apartment)* Hello?

REGGIE

What?

FRANK

I need some information about a....

REGGIE

He moved out.

FRANK

Who?

REGGIE

That guy. He moved out.

FRANK

You don't know who I'm talking about, sir.

REGGIE

Yes I do. The guy who moved out.

FRANK

Hello. Sir. If we could just for a moment discuss this guy who moved out so that we can determine that we're talking about the same guy? Sir? *(Tries another apartment)* Hello.

                    MAG
Sorry?

                    FRANK
I wonder if I could...

                    MAG
Sorry. No.

                    FRANK
...trouble you for a moment. Please. I'm looking for...

                    MAG
Sorry. Don't know him.

                    FRANK
...a man. I believe he lives in this building.

                    MAG
Don't know anybody on the fourth floor.

                    FRANK
Wait. I only want to ask a simple question.

                    MAG
Don't know anybody.

                    FRANK
A *simple question.*

                    MAG
Sorry.

                    FRANK
(*Pushing buttons*) Hello. Hello. Hello. What on earth is
wrong with all you people? Can't a person do a little
digging around without arousing all this *suspicion*? I can't
believe the level of paranoia here!

JACK

Come on up then, fella!

A buzzer signalling the opening of a door.

FRANK

Thank God for some people I always say. The ones who make you believe that goodness just might exist somewhere on this evil planet.

Pause.

JACK appears, smiling.

Or is it just that they want a friend?

JACK

Oh. I tell you. That was a big rat. That was a rat this big, I tell you. And I just hit it with that shovel there. And that split his head right open. Did I tell you about that?

FRANK

Four times. But never mind.

JACK

Yeah. That was a big fella.

FRANK

So tell me again about the man who lives down the hall.

JACK

Which one is that?

FRANK

The man I've asked you about repeatedly.

JACK

Oh, well. That guy. Yeah. Do I know that guy?

FRANK

He lives down the hall.

JACK

Did I see him going in and out? Or what?

FRANK

Well, it's hard to tell what you've seen and what you haven't, exactly.

JACK

I saw a rat. Big one. In the corner. I tell you.

FRANK

And what about the man? The one down the hall.

JACK

Not very friendly. That fella.

FRANK

No?

JACK

Mean-looking bastard.

FRANK

That's the one.

JACK

Cracked him over the head with that shovel.

FRANK

Who?

JACK

That big old rat. This big. Bigger. Excuse me. *(To imaginary friend)* Stay out of this. What? *(To FRANK)* Got a buddy here. Says he doesn't like you.

FRANK

Me? Why?

JACK

Don't know. Ask him.

FRANK

(Sighs, then speaks to JACK's friend) Why don't you like me?

JACK

(Sotto voce, to FRANK) He's kind of mental.

FRANK

Oh. Really?

JACK

Yeah. Laying hardwood floors. Forty years. Lot of glue.

FRANK

Does *he* know that man down the hall?

JACK

Better ask him.

FRANK

(Out) It's interesting how intimidated you can be by someone who isn't even there. I did, however, manage to decipher that the man down the hall was a Mr. Henry Walker, that he'd moved in about a month ago, that he'd never had anybody up to his room, that generally he didn't say much to his neighbours, and most importantly, that his garbage had been gone through by Jack here and his friend — I'm sorry...?

JACK

Jack.

FRANK

Would either of you care to tell me about it?

JACK

(Interpreting) Nothing much to tell, he says. Few crumpled up pieces of paper. An old light switch.

FRANK

Light switch?

JACK

Pizza box. About this big. No. About this big...

FRANK

(Out) They explained in a kind of odd detail, the entire contents of Mr. Walker's garbage. I decided to check it out for myself. Put things in a kind of order I could understand. And... (Taking out a notebook) ...I uncovered the following rather interesting items, among the refuse. Alphabetically: An *Advertiser Weekly*. Last month's. Indecipherable little notes. Kleenex with *blood* on it. And, get this — minute pieces of plastic electrical wire casing. Which would explain a lot — don't you think?

FINN

(In the newspaper office) Not your state of mind.

FRANK

The wire strippers. The guy is obviously reconnecting the electricity in some bizarre and specific way. Then there's that discarded light switch. And look at the types of food he eats. It all points to one thing.

FINN

An electrician with a bad diet.

FRANK

A stakeout, Mr Finn. And what about all this blood? No.
I've decided to leave town and I need your help.

FINN

You know I don't like to help people out.

FRANK

You're one of my only friends.

FINN

(Sympathetically) Really?

FRANK

I need to do one last gardening column. Apparently he's
one of the few people who bothers to read our paper.
(Away) It took some convincing, but finally Mr. Finn
agreed. I tried to write about something that would grab
Mr. Walker's attention. I wrote about the electrical wiring
of low-voltage garden lights. I made subtle reference to
him throughout with things like "Those who follow me
regularly will note," etc. etc. I said it was my last column
and that I was headed East for a while, when actually I
was headed West. And finally I referred to Mr. Walker by
name. And this is what I said.

WALKER & FRANK

(Appearing, reading the paper as FRANK disappears) If there's
a Mr. Henry Walker out there, I've got a little gardening
advice for him.

WALKER

"Quit digging around."

FINN

So?

31

                    WALKER
Quit digging around *what*?

                    FINN
Look. I hardly know the guy.

                    WALKER
He was an employee here for five years.

                    FINN
Five? Was he?

                    WALKER
Why are you protecting him?

                    FINN
I'm not. I wouldn't. What's he done?

                    WALKER
A lot of things.

                    FINN
Him?

                    WALKER
Why not?

                    FINN
He doesn't seem the type.

                    WALKER
Yeah? What type is that?

                    FINN
Unlikely.

                    WALKER
Those are usually the ones.

FINN

(Disappearing) They are?

WALKER

This Finn guy wasn't very co-operative.

ASTRID

(Appearing) Well...Frank's pretty nondescript. From what I can remember.

WALKER

(Out) Neither was that woman. No. *(Blowing his stack)* Not very co-operative at all!

ASTRID

Gosh. You seem so angry.

WALKER

Yeah? Well, life makes me angry.

ASTRID

Really?

WALKER

Look. Could you get me a Kleenex? I'm about to have a nosebleed here.

ASTRID

(Going off) Maybe you shouldn't get so emotionally involved in these things.

WALKER

Nobody seemed to know anything about this guy.

CLAYTON

(Entering) Maybe there was nothing to know.

WALKER
Don't give me that. They were lying. *Every one of them.*

CLAYTON
People don't lie. It takes too much imagination. They just generalize.

WALKER
I don't mind being misled, Clayton. It's not the dishonesty of people that makes me so mad. It's the completely dishonest way they go about it. If people are going to do things behind your back, they should at least...not...do them behind your back.

CLAYTON
Where'd you find all this moral integrity, Walker? In prison?

WALKER
(Enraged) You don't know anything about that! You hear me!?

CLAYTON
I bet I do.

WALKER
You could never know.

CLAYTON
I bet I could. Try me.

WALKER
All I ever wanted to do was get to the bottom of things.

CLAYTON
From what I understand, you went *right* to the bottom.

                    WALKER
Don't provoke me, Clayton.

                    CLAYTON
The truth can be a bloody nuisance, can't it, Walker?

                    WALKER
Oh, geez. Quick. My nose.

    WALKER steps forward into another scene.

    ASTRID appears with Kleenex from her bag.

                    ASTRID
Here.

                    WALKER
(Muffled) Thank you.

                    ASTRID
So are you a detective or something like that?

                    WALKER
Something like that.

                    ASTRID
I haven't gone out with Frank in a long time. I broke up
with him when I realized what was going on.

                    WALKER
What was going on?

                    ASTRID
Nothing. Do you have really high blood pressure? I have
practically no blood pressure at all.

WALKER
Did he belong to any organizations that you know of?

ASTRID
Frank?

WALKER
Did he have any political affiliations?

ASTRID
It seems to me he belonged to just about everything. He
had fourteen video rental cards or something. Six bank
accounts.

WALKER
Didn't you find that a little suspicious?

ASTRID
And he never entered any contests in case he might win.
Once, at some theatre thing, they dragged him up on
stage. Afterwards I had to take him to emergency with
chest pains. He didn't like to be singled out.

WALKER
Did he ever say why?

ASTRID
Probably.

WALKER
You don't know much about him.

ASTRID
(Realizing, wandering off) No. I don't.

CLAYTON
(Reappearing) Maybe she didn't.

WALKER

She knew. They all knew, but nobody was talking.

CLAYTON

Show me evidence of something. That's all I ask.

WALKER

He went through my garbage!

CLAYTON

How do you know that?

WALKER

It was all folded and organized by subject.

CLAYTON

Sure. So you decided to leave town.

WALKER

He was going East. I thought I'd go West.

CLAYTON

I thought you were after the truth, Walker?

WALKER

I was!

CLAYTON

Then why were you heading away from it?

WALKER

(Out) Sometimes in a person's life, they have to go where they have to go. So I went.

Bus station ambiance.

WALKER looks at his watch, checks the schedule, looks about impatiently, wanders off.

FRANK

(Entering) I always feel safer in a bus depot. The rate of crime is very high, but then so is the volume of traffic, so the chances of survival here are pretty good. So many other victims to choose from. Like sheep. You just need to keep quietly grazing. (He discovers the bloody Kleenex HENRY dropped on the floor from the previous scene.)

What's this? Oh, my God. Can it be? Blood! His! I just know it is. I've got to get out of here.

FRANK darts off as HENRY enters.

HENRY looks at his watch again, looks about, then wanders off in FRANK's direction.

The scene transforms to a cafe. Immediately, a waitress shows FRANK to a table. It's a very small table, with two small chairs —about three-quarter size.

FRANK

(Stopping in his tracks) It's so small.

JUNE

Take it or leave it.

FRANK

(Looking about) Don't you think it's a bit conspicuous?

JUNE

It's small. How can it be conspicuous? Big is conspicuous. Small is inconspicuous.

FRANK

People are already looking at me.

JUNE

What do you expect? You're making a fuss. Don't make a
fuss — people won't look at you. Sit down.

FRANK

(Handed a huge menu) Good heavens.

JUNE

What now?

FRANK

It's so *big.*

JUNE

What?

FRANK

Is it necessary that it be so big?

JUNE

It's exactly the same size as everyone else's.

FRANK

It is?

JUNE

All the menus are the same size. All the tables are the
same size.

FRANK

But couldn't the tables be a little bigger and the menus be
a little smaller? As a general rule? That's all I'm asking.

JUNE

Why don't you just order?

FRANK

(*Sotto voce*) Could you keep your voice down? Please. I
don't know what I want. I need a minute.

JUNE

Alright. A minute. *JUNE goes.*

FRANK

If I'm so "inconspicuous," why is everybody looking at me
now? I hate restaurants. I hate them. This always happens.

WALKER enters and FRANK quickly hides behind his menu.

JUNE

I suppose you want a table, too.

WALKER

(*Looking about*) A — a — table? Who wants to know?

JUNE

There aren't any.

WALKER

Oh. I'll wait.

JUNE

You have to wait. What?

WALKER

I'll wait.

JUNE

You're going to have to.

*JUNE heads back to FRANK's table. She pulls at the menu,
but FRANK is holding on.*

JUNE

What do you want?

FRANK

Wait. I need the menu. Don't take the menu. I haven't decided yet.

JUNE

There are hundreds of people waiting for tables.

FRANK

Hundreds? There's one. One!

JUNE

What's wrong with you?

FRANK

Nothing. Go away! Scat!

JUNE

You listen to me, mister. I'm a waitress here. I don't take orders from people.

FRANK

Quiet!

JUNE

Give me this menu and get the hell out of my restaurant!

FRANK

(Still struggling with the menu) This isn't your restaurant.

JUNE

Oh, yeah? What makes you such an authority?

FRANK

For heaven's sake — it happens to be one of an
international chain of restaurants of which I doubt very
much you are an owner in whole or in part.

JUNE

Oh. So I suppose you think I'm not going anywhere in life,
just because I'm stuck in here. Well, maybe I took a quick
look around and thought "Where the hell is everybody
trying to get to?" And I realized this was *it*. Hunh?

FRANK

I wonder if you could stop drawing quite so much
unnecessary attention to this table? As small as it is —
you've managed to make it loom very large.

JUNE

What are you hiding from?

FRANK

Please.

JUNE

You a convict?

FRANK

Really. Is it necessary to clear my record with you in order
to get service? Fine. I have no criminal convictions at the
moment. But thank you for asking. I'll have the Peter
Rabbit Salad.

JUNE

Bunny size or regular?

FRANK

Bunny please. And I'd like to keep the menu so that I can
peruse the desserts at my leisure, thank you.

JUNE

Oh, brother.

WALKER

(As JUNE passes) Excuse me.

JUNE

You again?

WALKER

(Indicating FRANK's table) There's an empty seat. Right there.

JUNE

(Pause) You have to *wait* to be seated.

WALKER

Well, I've waited and now I'd like to be seated.

JUNE

Oh, I see. Yeah. Everybody else has to wait, but not you, because you're different. You're on a special journey. Is that right? Just a second. *(Loudly announcing)* Ladies and gentlemen, there's a man here with a *bus* to catch! Could everybody else just *leave?* *(To WALKER)* There.

WALKER

Thank you.

JUNE goes, and WALKER, mortified, slinks over to FRANK's table, as FRANK hides behind his menu.

WALKER

Mind if I sit here?

FRANK

—

43

WALKER
(Shrugs. Pauses.) You suppose I could look at that menu?

FRANK
No comprende, señor.

WALKER
Yeah? What's that supposed to mean?

FRANK
(Affecting French) Pardon?

JUNE
(Returning with salad) Hey!

WALKER
(Very English pronunciation) La menu.

JUNE
Who told you to sit down?

WALKER
This guy doesn't mind.

JUNE
Him?

FRANK
(Yes I do.)

JUNE
I don't give a good goddamn what he thinks.

WALKER
As a matter of fact we were having a perfectly decent conversation, before you bull-dozed your way in here and rudely interrupted us.

JUNE

That's it! I've had enough. Get out! Everybody! Out! Out
of my restaurant! Now!

*JUNE whips the menu out of FRANK's hand, leaving him
and WALKER to face each other for a moment.*

WALKER & FRANK

You!

*Suddenly, FRANK tosses his salad at WALKER and makes a
run for it.*

WALKER

(Calmly taking out his notebook, he slowly makes note)
Definitely — up — to something. *(Putting away the
notebook)* But why? *(He slowly picks the lettuce off)* People
don't go through my garbage for no reason. Interview my
neighbours. Publish secret messages in the press. Taunt
me with mocking tongue gestures. Throw salad. *(He rises
and begins a journey, as the scene changes around him again
and again)* These are no accidents — these little — events
— in my life. From that day I was struck by lightning,
three years old, charred and dazed, staring up into the sky
and wondering what happened, I began to sense a certain
something about myself: that I was a sort of — a
conductor — of bad things. You know? That all the ill will
that could exist in the universe was somehow attracted to
me, drawn down through me like a kind of a lightning
rod. Just this — lone tree on the landscape. An orphan
from birth, left standing, just waiting for bad luck to strike
me. Sometimes it only happened in little, quiet ways. The
way ice cream falls off the cone. Just another dream lying
on the ground. Melting in the gutter. Or sometimes in
ways more excruciating. Those prospective parents at the

orphanage? Looking at me. Ugly. Ridiculous. Standing at the other end of the room. They'd never pick me. But how many times did they bring me out anyway, just to let me know. How many teachers would ignore my raised hand? How many prayers at night go unanswered? How many women charitably smile at me in bars. Hoping I wouldn't come over to chat. How many years pass me by—and how many chances—before I realized there was a kind of pattern to all of this. Life had always seemed to me a little like Bingo. You know: You keep playing, even though someone else is always winning. You don't think about the person calling the numbers. But then, you start to wonder. Gee. How many times can a guy possibly lose? How much bad luck? Bad timing? Bad news? Three broken engagements. Nine broken bones. Four laughable attempts at corrective surgery. One accidentally removed kidney. Three times attacked by animals at a wild game preserve (all in the same day). Five times fired. Eight, laid off. Bingo. Bingo. Twice electrocuted. Once loved. Accidentally. She thought I was someone else. So she says. For two weeks. I didn't know she was supposed to meet him on the corner. I happened to be there. Can you believe it was two weeks before she finally used his name? I can't. I went and lay down in the middle of the road. A car swerved and hit another car. Two people were seriously injured. Bingo. I once fell out of a small airplane on takeoff. Or was I pushed? Just rolled across the runway. And somehow into a cargo hold, unconscious. Flown to Resolute Bay with a consignment of medical supplies. Coincidence? Well, that's what they'd like you to think, isn't it? These people. The ones *he's* with. The ones calling all the numbers. The numbers that are never mine. These are my numbers here. *(With lottery ticket from wallet)* See. Every week I buy another lottery ticket, just to prove I'll never win. And I never will. I know it with the loss of every job. With every eviction. Every jail term. Oh, yes. Even that, on occasion. You see, I've finally become what

46

they intended. Over time. Lost my...civility, you might say. But then, how many lousy numbers can they call, before a guy finally goes after the caller?

Music interlude, during which we see FRANK and WALKER follow each other. Following this sequence, WALKER stands, suitcase in hand.

                    WALKER
Of course, I shouldn't expect people to really care. After all, isn't life complicated and difficult enough? Yeah — maybe. But *why* is it so complicated and difficult? Well. That's just the way the numbers come up, you think. Bingo. Nobody bothers to think about it.

The scene changes a little so that we see a repeat of the first bus stop scene with FRANK, now from WALKER's perspective.

And then by chance, one day standing at some bus stop, you happen to notice a stranger who somehow seems connected to something. Something of which you are a part. However unwittingly. He *seems* to be alone. Acting on his own. You might almost *believe* that he's just some nobody — just like you — working away at some pointless kind of — life. Maybe this *isn't* about anything, you begin to think, waiting for your bus. Maybe there *is* no higher order to things. No conspiracy of any kind. Just some runaway machine we're part of. Pistons wildly pumping, the speed accelerating, and no one at the controls. But then, out of the corner of your eye — you may suddenly catch a glimpse of the truth.

FRANK sticks out his tongue, as WALKER disappears.

A pause.

FRANK

(*Hitchhiking as he speaks*) And then he left. Abruptly. And
that was the beginning of that. My whole life just started
to just come away in pieces, like — like a rusty
automobile. My job. My fiancée. My sanity. And before I
knew it, I found myself at the side of the road, having left
my life back in some ditch somewhere, and I'm
hitchhiking — for God's sake. Well, I certainly had no
intention of travelling by the usual means. So instead I
was reduced to playing the sort of tattered vagabond —
taking refuge in the wild regions.

*A coyote howls, a look from FRANK, as the lights fade on
him, and go up on WALKER. and LAWRENCE.*

WALKER

(*Listening*) For a while, I felt sort of hopeful out there.
Miles of — possibilities. Fresh air. I'm at this truck stop.
Got a lift with this guy, Lawrence. His mind. Man. What
the road can do to you. Or maybe it was just the drugs he
was taking...

LAWRENCE

The *what*?

WALKER

You sure you're okay to drive now?

LAWRENCE

Man. I got some seconal in the truck. That'll bring me
down. Right down.

WALKER

What's your big hurry anyway?

LAWRENCE

Don't want to slow things down too much. *(With significance)* Might stop altogether. Wow. That's an awfully big June bug over there.

WALKER

That's a dog.

LAWRENCE

Whoa! Ugly dog, man.

WALKER

I don't think you should be handling an eighteen-wheeler in your condition.

LAWRENCE

It's only a road. It ain't like I'm driving to the moon or anything.

WALKER

I wouldn't be too sure about that.

LAWRENCE

It's just a line, man. One long, fuckin' line. From one end of the world to the other. Then back again. See ya!

WALKER

Thanks for the lift.

LAWRENCE *is gone.*

To nowhere. But never mind. I was just glad to be back on the road, again. And out in the open. There's a feeling you get when you leave something behind. Like maybe that thing never existed in the first place. *(Sound of a bus)* There must be some place, I thought, where these people can't follow me. And I was going to go there.

Sound of bus leaving. WALKER disappears in smoke.

Sound of truck air-horn. Lights up on LAWRENCE driving with FRANK in the passenger seat.

LAWRENCE
You ever think about two realities existing simultaneously? Like I'm going this way, and some guy's going the other way. All that's separating us is our direction, man.

FRANK
Do you think it's safe to pass?

LAWRENCE
And like this is the little yellow line, man, and what happens if it disappears, eh? Whoa! Nearly hit that fuckin' ship over there.

FRANK
Ship? That's a bus!

LAWRENCE
In the middle of a fuckin' canal?

FRANK
That's a road. That's a ditch! Look out.

LAWRENCE
For what?

FRANK
Let me out of here. Let me out!

LAWRENCE
Don't freak out, man. I'm licensed to do this.

FRANK

Just stop the truck. Stop the truck! I'll flag down that bus.
Gear down. Down. There. Down. Down.

LAWRENCE

Oops. What was that?

FRANK

Just a small mammal. Forget it.

LAWRENCE

(Upset) Aw.

FRANK

Watch the road!

LAWRENCE

Where?

FRANK

What do you mean, "where"? The road!

LAWRENCE

Hey! I know how to drive, man! I'm a member of the
fuckin' union!

Lights down on scene and up on bus.

*WALKER asleep on MONA's shoulder. She looks as if she
doesn't know what to do with the situation. He wakes with a
start.*

MONA

Bad dream?

WALKER

What?

51

MONA

Must've had a nightmare.

WALKER

(Quickly straightening himself) Oh. Yes. *(A pause as he registers MONA, gazing at him)*

MONA

Yeah. Your mouth was sort of twitching.

WALKER

(Out) I fell asleep on this lady's shoulder, you see. On this bus to nowhere. When I woke up it was raining, just softly raining on the window, see, and her scent was like the scent of cucumbers. I looked at her and I felt like crying all of a sudden. Maybe I felt the tears would relieve my eyes a little and help me see clearly what was up ahead. But I think buses are like life in a way. Someone else is driving. And you can only sit and watch the passing of it.

CLAYTON

(Appearing) Cut the crap, Walker.

MONA

That's like poetry, what you said.

WALKER

Maybe you just don't know what poetry *is*, Clayton.

CLAYTON

(Disappearing) I know what it *isn't*.

MONA

I love poetry. It's my favorite thing.

WALKER

What's your name, by the way?

MONA

It's Mona. It's a stage name.

WALKER

You must be an actress.

MONA

So, how did you guess? Theatre is my favorite thing.

CLAYTON

(Off) I thought poetry was her favorite thing.

WALKER

(To CLAYTON) So she had a *lot* of favorite things. *(Out)*
Then, she offered me a sandwich. I don't recall that
anyone has ever done that before.

MONA

I gave up meat but I keep forgetting. I had a bad
experience with a pork chop once.

WALKER

(Gazing into her eyes) I'm sorry to hear that.

MONA

Yeah. So — what else? *(Pause)* I acted in this play? I don't
remember the name of it. I was really good, but those
fucking guys — I said "I don't have to take this shit from
you." They weren't even paying anyways. Do you ever get
this feeling like you want to just crawl right out of your
skin? Like a snake? Leave it there? And slither away?
You're looking at me so weird. What's wrong?

WALKER

Did I slobber on you when I was sleeping? I do that
sometimes.

MONA

That's okay. I drool all over myself. Once — I was drooling
down the side of my mouth, but I didn't even know it. I
was watching T.V., and I was *so* into it. You know? And I
see this spittle coming down, you know? And I thought it
was a — a — praying mantis. Or something.

WALKER stretches.

MONA

(A little freaked) Holy cow! Why did you do that?

WALKER

What? I was stretching.

MONA

Gee. I thought you were angry.

WALKER

You'd know if I was angry. I get *very* angry.

MONA

Yeah? Did you ever kill anybody?

WALKER

No. I've never done that.

MONA

I did. I shot a guy. I didn't kill him, but nearly. I'm not
very good at communicating my feelings sometimes.
What's your name anyway?

WALKER

It's Walker. Henry Walker.

MONA

That's so poetic. Walker. So sad. Like someone on a road.

You know? Walking. Just — not running — but walking. A Walker.

                              WALKER
Or you could just call me Henry.

                              MONA
So what's your occupation — Henry?

                              WALKER
Pre-occupation. That's my occupation.

                              MONA
Mine too.

                              WALKER
I used to be an electrician. I didn't know about anything else. But I knew about that. When I looked at a room, I saw wiring. That's all. Didn't see the things in the room. Didn't even see the room. Just wiring. And when I looked at people I didn't understand them, because I didn't see them. But now I think I see. This isn't just happening, Mona. There's a mechanism. Some kind of wheels turning here, somewhere. People don't see it because everybody's got their own little specialized compartment. You. Me. Everybody.

                              MONA
Yeah. I know. I got to go somewhere. I got to get out of my situation. I saw this psychic, right? Wait. I'll give you her address.

                              WALKER
Me?

                              MONA
(Writing out the address on an old ticket stub and giving it to

him) She's a genius. She said I'm going to go out into the world and take it on. Here. This is her card. See. "Directions charted." She said "Head East," so that's where I'm headed.

                        WALKER
East?

                        MONA
Is that a problem? Shouldn't I go there?

                        WALKER
Well, no. It's just that we're heading West.

                        MONA
Maybe I'll head to the mountains then.

                        WALKER
These *are* the mountains. Maybe you should check with somebody.

                        MONA
I don't even know where I really want to go, so who's going to tell me how to get there?

                        WALKER
Well. Maybe you should just go wherever you're going. Mona.

                        MONA
What about my acting career?

                        WALKER
I understand.

                        MONA
I've got to take the world on.

WALKER

We could both take it on. Stop being pushed around. We could do a little pushing. Start looking ahead and stop looking behind us all the time, just in case some... *(He looks around and sees FRANK, then quickly turns back)* Oh my God.

MONA

What? What is it?

WALKER

Don't look!

MONA

What?

WALKER

There's a man. Don't look. Sitting over there. Don't look!

MONA

What guy is this?

WALKER

Following me.

MONA

Following you? Why?

WALKER

That's him alright.

MONA

Him? He got on the bus while you were sleeping. He was out there in the middle of nowhere.

WALKER

Of course he was.

MONA

Don't worry. I'll take care of it.

WALKER

What?

MONA

I have this. *(Reaches into her purse)*

WALKER

What's that?!

MONA

A gun.

WALKER

Well, no. We can't kill him. Where'd you get that?

MONA

I took it from this movie set. I was an extra in this movie?

WALKER

Just...put it back in your bag and forget about it. *Don't* —
look back at him.

MONA

What'll we do now?

WALKER

Next stop? We make a run for it.

*Lights up on FRANK, as the lights go down on MONA and
WALKER.*

FRANK

(With a kind of detached assessment) I assumed they were
talking about me, since they kept looking back in my

direction. I assumed the discussion involved some sort of plan, of which I was, I assumed, an integral part. But if they assumed that I would fall into some trap of theirs, then they assumed wrong.

CLAYTON
(*Appearing*) That's a lot of assumptions, Frank.

FRANK
Is it?

CLAYTON
For such an unassuming guy.

FRANK
What's that? Is that a joke?

CLAYTON
So why did you get off the bus when they got off the bus? If you were trying to get away from them.

FRANK
Let's put it this way. Under the circumstances, it seemed appropriate.

CLAYTON
What circumstances are those, Frank?

FRANK
It was the last stop.

Scene changes back to MONA and WALKER, as FRANK fades.

MONA
Wait. What happens to us?

WALKER

Us? Who?

MONA

You're all I have, Mr. Henry Walker.

WALKER

(Aside) I didn't think it was possible that there could be
someone more desperate in the world than me. More
lonely. It made me love her. As much as my life will allow
me to love anyone. But then I thought about how it would
end. *(To MONA)* There'll be some kind of tragedy.

MONA

I love tragedy.

WALKER

You'll get sucked into a large engine of some kind, or
maybe crushed by a garbage compactor. Fall off a
mountain, while I'm taking your picture.

MONA

Oh.

WALKER

Don't you see, Mona, that you're as fated in life as I am?
Bad luck is my only companion. Let's not give anyone else
the pleasure of destroying our friendship, when we can
have the pleasure of ending it ourselves. Here and now.

MONA

Like in a French movie I saw.

They gaze into one another's eyes for a moment.

A pause.

                         WALKER
In a way it was one of the few fulfilling minutes of my life.
And then she got off the bus. But he didn't. It was the last
stop, but he just sat there.

                         FRANK
Waiting for me.

                         WALKER
Watching me.

                         FRANK
Then all of a sudden...

                    FRANK & WALKER
...we both headed for the door.

    They ram into one another.

                    FRANK & WALKER
Oh. Excuse me.

    They hurry off in opposite directions.

    Music.

    MONA appears, with a gun, and follows FRANK.

                         WALKER
(Returning) But he went off in *her* direction. Now I wonder
if she's in any danger?

    *Transition to MILLIE the psychic's place. During the whole
    scene, SERGIO, an unpleasant-looking sailor, stands to one
    side, whittling things with a knife.*

                           61

MILLIE

Danger. What is danger? *You* are in danger. Yes?

WALKER

You're some kind of a psychic I understand. See. Here.
(Hands her something)

MILLIE

B - 4?

WALKER

It's a ticket stub. She wrote your address on the back.

MILLIE

Okay. Just a second. *(She talks into her head as if it's a
telephone receiver)* Yeah. What? *(Back to normal)* That's
what I thought. Some liver things. You got some kind of
liver...problem?

WALKER

Kidney.

MILLIE

That's right. *(Looking at his palm)* I see a kidney.

WALKER

No. It's missing.

MILLIE

Yes. I see that it's missing. Hello? Damn — that line. Some
old energy field out there — I'm picking up. *(A shop bell)*
Wait! What is that sound I hear?

WALKER

The front of the shop.

FRANK

(From off) Hello! Is anybody home?

MILLIE

You are very perceptive. *(To SERGIO)* Sergio!

SERGIO opens his switchblade.

MILLIE

Wait. *(Going)* I go. Sergio is kind of shy about people.

WALKER

(Out) We stared at each other for about five minutes. And
in spite of how threatening he seemed, I wasn't the least
bit frightened of him. It's the knives you don't see in this
world you have to watch out for.

MILLIE returns.

FRANK

(From off)...I feel better already.

MILLIE

(Sitting again) A satisfied customer. Now. Where was I
here? Right. I sense a journey. A long journey. But where?

WALKER

I don't know.

MILLIE

So why don't you? *(Poking him)* Does that hurt?

WALKER

Ow! What about this guy who's following me?

MILLIE

Some guy is following you?

63

                    WALKER
You're the psychic.

                    MILLIE
Wait. I see some guy following you.

                    WALKER
That's the one.

                    MILLIE
Okay, well that must be why you cross the path that girl.
Mona. I tell her to head East.

                    WALKER
She was heading West.

                    MILLIE
Never mind all the directional semantics. East. West. Is the
same. This way. This way. The future is where you going
to end up — no matter what — cause you already there.
It's kind of dark European fatalism, you know. Is why
everybody smokes cigarettes over there. Yeah? Okay. I
thought so. It's a sheep. Some kind of black sheep on the
horizon.

                    WALKER
What? In a pasture?

                    MILLIE
Who knows? A mystery. What's this? Never mind. Just
some lottery numbers. Those guys. And that's old
numbers anyway from last week.

                    WALKER
His name is Frank Gardener. If that's any help.

                    MILLIE
You know him?

                    WALKER

I know his name.

                    MILLIE

And yet you're afraid.

                    WALKER

These people are serious. They've pushed me to the very
edge.

                    MILLIE

There is still some distance left to go.

                    WALKER

What can you tell me about this guy?

                    MILLIE

What do you want to know? It's blue. It's got some clouds
in it. It's the sky.

                    WALKER

No. **This — guy**. The one who's following me. Where will
I finally meet him in the end?

                    MILLIE

Meet. You don't want to meet. No. That's — danger — and
— maybe even det.

                    WALKER

Debt? Like I'm going to borrow some money? What?

                    MILLIE

No. Like dropping det.

                    WALKER

So that's it. Bingo. They're finally going to do me in.

MILLIE

I got some signals crossing here. Wow. What's all this? It's a kind of rittle.

WALKER

Rittle? Riddle!

MILLIE

Listen. The rittle. "Fear will follow you to the ends of the earth."

WALKER

That's forever. There is no end. It just goes around. The earth. And around.

MILLIE

But you reach the end when you come to the seashore. Isn't that right?

WALKER

The sea? Yes. Maybe that's it.

MILLIE

Maybe. Who knows?

WALKER

(Pause) I'll sail away then.

MILLIE

To where?

WALKER

Does it matter?

MILLIE

And yet I have a sense of something. A new destiny for you. "So long as the setting sun never sinks into the sea." This is the communication I'm getting.

WALKER

I'll have to head West and just keep heading there. Around and around and around the world. Is that what that means?

MILLIE

Yes. I think so.

WALKER

That way the sun will never sink.

MILLIE

(Gives a look to SERGIO) Yes. I see.

WALKER

How do I know you're right about all this?

MILLIE

How do you know I'm wrong?

Music. MILLIE fades away.

WALKER

(Out) I took her advice anyway, and I headed towards the sea. Sergio managed to overcome his shyness and follow me for a few miles, without saying anything. Then he pointed off towards the West, where I could see, glinting in the sunlight, a cargo ship. A black one. As if it had been waiting for me all along. Now the setting sun would never sink into the sea for me. I thanked him, but he didn't say a word. Just indicated that he wanted to bum a cigarette. Then he offered me the crucifix he was wearing in exchange. And it gave me an idea. I would give him my identity. *(Handing over his wallet to SERGIO)* It was perfect. Who would ever know? So we traded lives right there and then, this illegal immigrant and me. I gave him

67

my wallet and everything in it. Little did he realize where my destiny would lead him. *(Smiling for the first time)* I almost felt bad.

WALKER and SERGIO disappear in opposite directions.

MONA enters the bus depot men's room, with a gun at FRANK's back.

MONA
In here buddy!

FRANK
(Hands in the air) This is the men's room, by the way.

MONA
(The gun shaking all over the place) Now listen — I'm not very good at communicating, okay?

FRANK
The gun doesn't help.

MONA
Shut up! I know what you are. I know what's going on here. So — who are you!? And what's going on here!? Shut up! What are you after?

FRANK
After? It's *you* people that are after *me!*

MONA
(Letting down her guard) What people?

FRANK
(Out) When I told her the truth about him, she went completely berserk.

MONA

(Hysterical) Why did he lie to me!?

FRANK

Please put the gun down.

MONA

Men are such fuckin' liars! I could kill them *all*!!

FRANK

(Nervously sort of kneeling in deference to the gun) Wait! Not all men are bad. What about — priests? *(Short pause)* On second thought...What about — me? I'm a perfectly decent person. I've never treated any woman badly.

MONA

How do I know that?

FRANK

I hardly even *qualify* as a man. I do my own ironing. I'm too *neat and tidy*. Too *worried*. I'm sort of half-man, half....gelatin. You can't kill *me*. It would be like murdering — nothing.

MONA

(Weakening) How can you be so pathetic?

FRANK

It takes years of grovelling.

MONA

You in the talent agent business, by any chance?

FRANK

Me? Why? Are you looking for representation?

MONA

Maybe.

FRANK
Rather odd way of finding it.

MONA
My movie career's going nowhere. I keep getting turned
around.

FRANK
You're like me. Both of us — need to be ruthless about
where we're going in life, or we'll never get there.

MONA
Yeah. I know.

FRANK
(*Suddenly, out*) She wanted me to be her agent. I couldn't
see a future in it. For either of us. But somehow we parted
as friends. (*Back to MONA*) Stick to shooting movies.

MONA gives the gun to FRANK.

She gave me this as a kind of memento, and said:

MONA & FRANK
I hope it comes in handy.

Transition to travel agency.

FRANK
But I'm rather hoping it doesn't.

LEWIS
Just try not to point it *directly* at my head, okay? Thanks.

FRANK
Sorry. (*Waving the gun around. Out*) I'd never carried a
gun before.

LEWIS
(*Ducking*) Where am I booking you to?

FRANK
To where are you booking me.

LEWIS
I don't know.

FRANK
Someplace — obscure...

LEWIS
South Yemen?

FRANK
...that I can reach without a camel, thanks. An island.

LEWIS
Let's see. There are a few in French Polynesia that haven't
been blown up. Yet.

FRANK
Nothing — safer?

LEWIS
The Falklands?

FRANK
Less — controversial?

LEWIS
Elba.

FRANK
Too much history.

LEWIS

Galapagos.

FRANK

Too much biology.

LEWIS

The Hebrides?

FRANK

No trees.

LEWIS

South Moresby.

FRANK

Too many.

LEWIS

You really *do* want to get away. Here's something. Oh, I don't think you want to go *there*. Oh, no.

FRANK

Really? I'll take it.

LEWIS

(Disappearing) It's practically impossible to get to, you know.

FRANK

Perfect. *(Out)* Some island. I set out for a new life, somewhere beyond the shores of this one. Stopping for directions in one of those peculiar little seaside towns, where the people are as odd as the fish they catch. And about as warm-hearted. But never mind. I was armed now. Dangerous. Sort of. I was becoming a little dishevelled in appearance. I couldn't help noticing myself in a shop window as I passed it.

ALICE
(Appearing at the top of the stairs) Willy!

FRANK
I thought I was someone else. I really did. It was a strange
little shop, by the way. But it said in the window
"Directions charted," so I figured they sold maps. I went
in.

Bell.

FRANK
Hello. Is anybody home? *(Looking about)* Dear me.

MILLIE enters.

Then a woman entered from the back.

MILLIE
What do you want?

FRANK
I'm looking for directions. An island. *(Out)* She looked
me over once then said:

FRANK & MILLIE
I know that.

FRANK
You do?

MILLIE
This is psychic shop.

FRANK
I thought you sold maps.

                              MILLIE
Don't need map. I see that you are on a journey.

                              FRANK
Well, I told you that.

                              MILLIE
Don't need to tell. Wait! I see something. And then I see
something more.

                              FRANK
What?

                              MILLIE
Nothing.

                              FRANK
I thought you said you saw something.

                              MILLIE
Yes. Something, then nothing. *(With WALKER's ticket stub)*
Wait. I see a letter "B" and a number "4." You know
what's that?

                              FRANK
B - 4?

                              MILLIE
Before. Yes. And nothing after. It's kind of a threshold, I
think. And beyond is vast — what? Emptiness. Got to
watch your step. Take this. Something to remind always
look *before* you, not behind.

                              FRANK
A ticket stub? To what?

                              MILLIE
(Going off) Exactly.

                              74

FRANK

Well gosh — *(Calling after her)* — I feel better already. *(Leaving the shop)* B. 4. Always look be-fore me. Okay. So where's this threshold with nothing beyond? God, I hate psychics.

FRANK exits, tentatively, with ticket stub.

ALICE

(More insistently) Willy! Willy!

Lights up on a scene at sea, on board a cargo ship.

EDUARDO

Who are you?

WALKER

No one. Understand?

EDUARDO

(Pause) I understand. That is the crucifix that I gave to Sergio. Now it is yours.

WALKER

—

EDUARDO

Now *you* are my friend. Understand?

WALKER

Who says I'm looking for a friend?

They both look out to sea.

EDUARDO
I sense that you are sad.

WALKER
Why should I be sad? He's standing at the edge of the
world somewhere, and I'm sailing away off the end of it.
I'm out of his reach now. There's nothing — to fear.

EDUARDO
Nothing — is something to fear. And anyway, an enemy is
as good as a friend in lonely times. Where will you go,
now that you no longer have any reason to go there?

WALKER
Across this ocean, and the next one — to where the
"setting sun never sinks into the sea."

EDUARDO
(Crossing himself) La Puesto del Sol. Si.

Silence.

WALKER
Isn't that the name of this ship?

EDUARDO
(Intake of breath) Si. La puesto del sol. "The setting sun."

EDUARDO leaves the deck.

WALKER watches him go. Gazes out again. Thunder.
WALKER faces out, as the wind picks up.

ALICE
(A little panicked) Willy. Where are you?

WILLY

(*Appearing*) Where else would I be?

ALICE

Terrors are turned upon me, Willy. They pursue my soul as the wind tonight.

WILLY

Shall I get you some Ovaltine?

They disappear.

Foghorn.

Lights up on FRANK and a FERRYMAN. FRANK's nervous voice echoing in the mist.

FERRYMAN

This here is it.

FRANK

Oh, my.

FERRYMAN

Don't expect to come back this way though.

FRANK

Why not?

FERRYMAN

Last run. Government's cutting back on services.

FRANK

Perhaps you could recommend a little hotel somewhere? (*Pause*) A bed and breakfast?

FERRYMAN

Big white house up that-a-way. Up the road a-ways and over. By the sea. Shutters banging away in the breeze. Old rusty gate. House sits on a very high cliff. Some years ago, part of it fell right away and into the sea. Just like that. Some day soon the other half will follow.

FRANK

Have they thought of bringing in a structural engineer?

FERRYMAN

Woman up there. Flighty as a finch. And her blind friend. Queer ones. Sittin' like death. Waitin'. God only knows why. Nothing out here to wait for. Except the howling wind.

FRANK

Gosh. I wonder if I've come to the right place.

FERRYMAN

This? This here is the ends of the earth.

FRANK

Oh. Then I suppose I have.

Thunder. Music. Sound of waves.

Lights fade. Music swells.

End of Act One

Interval

Act Two

Music. The set has turned itself into a rotted, old, run-down hotel called "The Ends of the Earth," once in its heyday in the 1940s or 50s. Well, not really in its heyday ever. Nature has slowly begun to reclaim the furnishings. Things fall from the ceiling, collapse under foot, or come apart in the hand.

WILLY, a woman of simple thoughts, enters with FRANK in tow. Voices echo here, as if at the bottom of a barrel. WILLY is confused about directions, and seems to be able to make a terrible crowd out of two people.

FRANK

I think I'm going to try to find a real estate agent in the morning.

A look from WILLY.

There's always one of those — somewhere. I was actually thinking of a small stone cottage, by the water. I could do a lot of — catching up on things. Think of all the catching up I can do. And gardening, of course. Good heavens. And maybe even write a short story. Or a short novel. Or — a — long one. *(Pause)* Perhaps a *very* long one.

79

(Trailing off, he looks around him, really taking in the decay for the first time) Oh. *(Polite pause)* Maybe there's something else up the road. *(Starts to leave)*

WILLY
(Grabbing FRANK and pulling him into the room) Don't be put off by the complete lack of hospitality. Here. Sign the book.

FRANK
I said... *(Trapped)* ...oh. *(Blowing dust from a guest register)* Yes. I see you don't get a lot of — not since — good heavens. *(Pause)* Of course ferry service being what it is now.

WILLY
What is it?

FRANK
Nonexistent.

WILLY
Are you?

FRANK
Am I what?

WILLY
(Suddenly leading the way) This way.

FRANK
Which way? Oh. *(Following WILLY)* Am I what? I'm sorry. I missed the point there.

WILLY
Caught a later one, did you?

                    FRANK
Later? What?

                    WILLY
Never mind. Here you are.

                    FRANK
Yes. I am.

                    WILLY
Is that right?

                    FRANK
Is what right?

                    WILLY
Is what right?

                    FRANK
I'm sorry. You lost me.

                    WILLY
Where?

                    FRANK
Look. I'm not following this at all.

                    WILLY
Following what?

                    FRANK
This. Not at all.

                    WILLY
The whole situation is terribly confusing.

                    FRANK
I'd say so.

                    WILLY
But one grows accustomed to anything.

                            FRANK
Well, I think...

                    WILLY
Tea?

                            FRANK
Tea?

                    WILLY
At this hour?

                            FRANK
Pardon?

                    WILLY
(Going) I'll see what I can do.

                            FRANK
But I don't want any tea. I didn't say anything about tea.
Thanks.

                    WILLY
Oh, don't mention it.

    WILLY goes off.

                            FRANK
I didn't. Did I? Tea? It was one a.m. Well, terrific. I was on
an island I couldn't get off. Truly a "threshold with
nothing beyond." Really — an ideal setting. For a destitute
end. Or a life of cheery simple-mindedness. Which seemed
to be a bit of a local specialty. Why not have tea? I was
looking be-fore me now.

Thunder and lightning.

Oh. Thank you. Atmosphere. Perfect.

Plaster falls nearby. FRANK pulls out ticket stub.

Well anyway — I had this — ticket stub, so, in spite of everything else, I felt — *(Another piece of plaster falls, as he moves to avoid it)* — I had a place here.

CLAYTON appears.

CLAYTON
That's sarcasm, right?

FRANK
Honestly, Clayton. You act as if you don't believe a word I've been saying.

CLAYTON
It's no act.

FRANK
Well, what on earth's the point of my going on like this? I might as well not waste my breath.

CLAYTON
Oh — I find that people have a habit of lying their way to the truth...

FRANK
Not me.

CLAYTON
...eventually.

FRANK

So that's the game, is it?

CLAYTON

It's no game.

FRANK

Wear me down. Get me to say things.

CLAYTON

What things?

FRANK

Look. The situation was fraught with — odd
complications. Naturally, I didn't feel entirely at ease.

CLAYTON

You'd made your getaway.

FRANK

Yes, but — why would he follow me and then suddenly
not follow me?

CLAYTON

That's what I'd like to know.

*They give each other a look, as WILLY re-enters, and
CLAYTON disappears.*

WILLY

(With tea things tottering on tray) Here we are!

FRANK

Let me give you a hand with that.

                    WILLY
Why don't you give me a hand with this?

                    FRANK
What? No. I was going to give you a hand with that.

  Somehow he's in her way.

                    WILLY
Just sit down. Sit down. I'll do it myself.

                    FRANK
For heaven's sake.

  He sits down. The chair collapses on one side.

Ah!

                    WILLY
Oh. Look at that.

                    FRANK
That's fine, I'm — fine. *(Sighs)* Thank you.

                    WILLY
Why, it's right there in front of you, Mr. Travers.

                    FRANK
What is?

                    WILLY
Cream. And sugar.

                    FRANK
I said "Thank you."

                    85

                            WILLY
You're welcome.

                            FRANK
(Ever-so-politely) Are you deaf by any chance?

                            WILLY
Just a little ahead of myself. Let it steep, first.

                            FRANK
Steep?

                            WILLY
Oh. Just wait. I'll see what I can find.

                            FRANK
What?

    WILLY goes off.

    *We see blind ALICE in the shadows with an ax. She says
    nothing.*

                            FRANK
Oh, good grief! Is there nobody else around here — with
whom — one can — communicate — or is that simply too
much to ask!?

    *ALICE disappears again, as WILLY reappears with an armful
    of tea towels and a tablecloth.*

                            WILLY
This all the linen there is, I'm afraid.

                            FRANK
Oh. Thank you.

She hands the linen to him.

WILLY

No one's done any washing of any kind.

FRANK

Yes, well. Perhaps just put them down.

WILLY

Take them. Take them. Why not? It's every man for himself.

FRANK takes them.

WILLY sits. A moment passes. She smiles.

WILLY

What?

FRANK

What? *(Pause)* Why did you say "What"?

WILLY

(Looking into the teapot with a flashlight) We all have to help each other out around here.

FRANK

Really?

WILLY

No. Not quite. Another minute. *(Offering)* Biscuit?

FRANK

(Trying to reach) Perhaps if I put these down.

WILLY

Yes. Take those. Why not?

FRANK

(Taking biscuit) Never mind. Thank you. *(Looking)* Oh, dear.

WILLY

It's alright.

FRANK

These are bouillon cubes.

WILLY

Take two.

FRANK

Thank you. One'll be...Mmm.

WILLY

Oh, just slightly.

FRANK

I thought so.

WILLY

And you?

FRANK

Not completely. But I'm getting there.

WILLY

Oh. Well, give me your cup then.

FRANK

Thank you.

WILLY pours, but nothing comes out.

WILLY

You like it strong, I hope.

FRANK

A little stronger than that, actually.

WILLY

Sugar?

FRANK

Uh, I think this is cornstarch.

WILLY

Oh, dear. Well, I hope someone gets some more.

FRANK

I said "I think this is cornstarch"!

WILLY

Ha. Ha. Really? And what did *you* say?

FRANK

I said "**I — think — this — is — corn — starch.**"

WILLY

Oh. *(Pause)* I don't get it.

FRANK

Neither do I.

WILLY

It's been such a long time since anyone else was here.

FRANK

Even longer than that, I imagine.

WILLY

I suppose you'd like to see a room.

FRANK

What? Now?

WILLY

Oh. Well, alright. *(She rises)*

Suddenly, a knock on the ceiling.

WILLY

(Dead silence, and then ever-so-quietly) Oh. It's Alice. She's not very fond of visitors, as you can see. *(Rising, WILLY heads for the stairs)*

FRANK

(Following) Alice? Is she someone I should — ? Alice? Does she run this place? Is this registering with you at all?

WILLY

I'm beginning to wonder, myself.

FRANK

Yes.

WILLY

(Stops, out of wind, confused) Soap. What about the soap?

FRANK

...can I give you a hand up the stairs, or something?

WILLY

Perhaps you could give me a hand here?

WILLY heads down.

FRANK

Do other people find you as confusing as I do?

WILLY

Do they?

FRANK

Which way are you going?

WILLY

Oh, that's alright then. You go on up ahead. But be careful.
We're a few steps short of a stairway.

FRANK

Yes. I'd say so.

She disappears again. As FRANK speaks, he wanders up the
stairs.

FRANK

While she went off in search of — whatever, I ventured to
the top of the stairs, what there was of them, and down an
endless corridor. As accommodation goes, it wasn't. Really
more like an unpleasant corner of the mind. Doors to
forgotten things. Each one slightly ajar, so that I could just
make out the contents. Such dreadful little rooms.
Dilapidated hovels, really. Each the size of a closet. There
weren't even any beds that I could see. At the very end of
the hall I saw a door that was shut, however. Was there
another guest? I went up and quietly knocked. No answer.
I reached for a doorknob, but it came off in my hand.
Suddenly I heard a woman's voice behind me.

ALICE & FRANK

Go!

FRANK

Is all it said. *(Shivers)* I took it as a sort of — hint. *(He*
disappears.)

91

Thunder and lightning. After a few moments, a loud echoing knock.

Downstairs again, WILLY appears. After a second knock and more lightning and thunder, the door creaks open and we see the shadow of a man slowly stretch across the room.

WILLY

Oh. What on earth are you doing out there?

WALKER

Where? Where am I?

WILLY

(With a roll of toilet paper) Here's the soap, then. It's all I could find.

WALKER

(Entering, all wet, in a daze) Thank you. We went down. I thought — but...

WILLY

No — you ought to go on back up. You'll catch your death.

WALKER

My death, yes. If only. But there's no escaping them. My God. They've even conspired with the sea against me. And the setting sun — sank.

CLAYTON

But you saved yourself from drowning?

WALKER

I didn't save myself, Clayton. Somehow *they* did. It's all part of the plan. Don't you see? There I am, crawling out of the waves, onto a beach. How? Climbing this cliff. I see this house, half-fallen into the sea. They won't find me here. Then I look up. And hanging by a rusty nail there's this sign, this old sign swinging wildly in the wind, suddenly coming loose and striking me to the ground. I look. And there it is. The hotel name. "The Ends of the Earth." Everything that woman said came true. This was *meant* to happen. Their plan isn't to kill me. They want to drive me mad.

                    WILLY
Yes.

                    WALKER
What?

                    CLAYTON
So why didn't you just let yourself slip quietly into the water? Escape them forever?

                    WALKER
Maybe I don't *want* freedom, Clayton.

                    WILLY
How about a sandwich, then?

                    WALKER
Huh?

                    WILLY
(Going) I'll see what I can find, Mr. Travers. But don't expect me to wait on you hand and foot.

                    WALKER
Sandwich? Did I say "sandwich"? *(His nose starts bleeding)*

CLAYTON

So — if you don't want freedom, what *do* you want, Walker?

WALKER

(Using toilet paper on his nose) Knowledge. I need to know why they're doing this.

Plaster falls.

What is this place? Where did she go? I don't want a sandwich, I — Mr. Travers? I'm not Mr. Travers. I don't even *know* a Mr. Travers. Or do I? *(Finds guest register)* There hasn't been anybody here since — wait a minute. Someone arrived tonight. *(Looking upstairs, then going off after WILLY)* Hello? Ma'am?

FRANK enters from upstairs, with doorknob.

FRANK

Hello! *(Part of the banister comes away in his hand)* Ah! Hello!? Where is it I'm supposed to sleep, exactly? I'm afraid this doorknob has...hello? *(Descending the stairs, cautiously)* Hello? Where is that — fruit bat of a woman anyway? Fell through the floor...one can only guess. *(Looking around, he sees a door)* I decided to poke around. Here was a door I hadn't opened. *(With doorknob)* And I have just the equipment to do it. *(Pausing for a moment to listen)* No dire warnings from anyone. *(He opens the door)*

ALICE emerges with a large pair of scissors. Music up full, and FRANK faints, falling hidden from view. ALICE disappears into the closet and WILLY reappears with WALKER behind.

94

WALKER

(*Secretively*) This gentleman. Your other guest. This Mr.
Travers. Does he happen to be a slimy little weasel with a
phony moustache, by any chance?

WILLY

(*With a sandwich on a plate*) There's one at the end of the
hall.

WALKER

I thought so.

CLAYTON

So you decided that you'd kill him right then and there?

WALKER

I know how this works, Clayton. You take my own words
and turn them around so that before I realize it, I'm
confessing to a murder.

CLAYTON

You are?

*As WALKER disappears up the stairs, WILLY looks about for
him.*

FRANK wakes.

FRANK

Ah.

WILLY

Ah!

FRANK

My God. Who was that?

WILLY
(*Offering sandwich*) Do you plan on waking early?

FRANK
If at all. Oh. Thank you. That's — (*Taking the sandwich, as he continues*) — very nice. Lovely.

WILLY
Might you need an alarm clock? (*Rummages through the closet, where ALICE has just been*)

FRANK
Wait, there's someone — where did she go? She was right there. Really. This dreadful, horrible-looking, nightmare of a — (*Turning around face-to-face with ALICE*) Ah! Good heavens! You surprised me. (*Catching his breath*) Good evening. (*Extending a hand*) The name is Miles. Travers. And you must be...?

ALICE extends her hand in a very slow and odd way, rather slothlike and disconnected to her body. FRANK shakes her hand while he speaks, but it's clearly a disturbing experience.

I guess I'll be staying here tonight, and tomorrow I'll be — well — I'm not really sure about tomorrow. I've been through a lot, really, in the last couple of months. To tell you the truth, I've had a sort of nervous breakdown, I guess you could say.

ALICE walks down toward the tea things and he follows.

So I sort of decided to leave it all behind, as they say. Look for something — quieter. Although I have to admit I find this part of the world — for me — exceedingly quiet. (*A pause*) Are you associated with the hotel in any way? Are you "Alice," by any chance? The one who isn't very fond of — yes. Well. *(Pause. He bites into the sandwich)* Mmm. That's rather... *(He falls silent trying to understand what he's eaten)*

ALICE
Willy has an odd way of running things.

FRANK
Really?

ALICE
She seems to like guests.

FRANK
(Politely removing an oven mitt from his mouth) !

ALICE
Personally, I don't like people at all.

FRANK
Ah. Well — that would explain the sharp objects.

ALICE
That's why I came here in the first place. Not a lot of other visitors.

FRANK
I thought maybe you ran the place.

ALICE
In case you hadn't noticed, I'm blind.

FRANK
I see. I mean...sorry. I didn't mean "see," literally. What I meant was —

ALICE
You'll find the management incompetent at best. Willy

likes people, yet goes out of her way to do nothing for them. You won't enjoy staying here at all. I think you should *both* leave before it's too late.

FRANK

Both?

ALICE

(*Wandering off*) You and the other gentleman.

FRANK

Oh dear. Is that who's at the end of the hall?

ALICE

You mustn't go in there.

FRANK

I was only curious.

ALICE

There's no *room* for curiosity in this place. Do you understand?

CLAYTON

(*Appearing*) So she told you.

FRANK

Told me?

ALICE

No room.

ALICE *is gone.*

FRANK

She didn't tell me anything. All I knew was that there was no *room* for — no — room? Oh, my God. That's it! The

threshold. Beyond which that psychic saw nothing. Of
course. *(Gives a look up the stairs)* And didn't that
unpleasant ferry worker say that half the house had fallen
into the sea?

                         CLAYTON
So you figured it out.

                         FRANK
But then where was this other gentleman? The one who
had left a bloody tissue on the — My God! It's him. *(Picks
up the bloody tissue)* I've got to get out of here or I'm done
for? How did he find this place? It's not even on the map.
My God these people are well-organized.

                         CLAYTON
Organized?

                         FRANK
How else?

                         CLAYTON
Gee. That's crazy, Frank. That's paranoia.

                         FRANK
Maybe. But paranoia is, after all, just a concept. Invented
by — whom?

                         CLAYTON
Paranoids?

                         FRANK
Think about it. What is sanity, Clayton? And who defines
its boundaries? The system. There's something in all of us
they want to destroy. A thought we had once. Like a weed
popping up through a crack in the pavement. Some
thought. We step out of line for a moment and there we
are.

WILLY

(Appearing) Mr. Travers!

FRANK

Huh?

WILLY

(Descending) You're all over the place recently.

FRANK

I'm right here.

WILLY

Where?

FRANK

Here.

WILLY

You're right here.

FRANK

That's what I said. Didn't I say that?

WILLY

Can't sleep, is that it? Hot milk.

FRANK

No. Please. (Please!)

WILLY

(Going) Won't be a minute.

FRANK

Please!

ALICE

(Appearing) She won't listen to you.

FRANK

(*Startled*) Oh, my God — you certainly know how to frighten a person.

ALICE

She just couldn't care less what's being said. Willy tends to answer questions no one has even asked yet. There's a certain hypnotic inevitability about it. She likes to trap people in confusion — so that she's the only one who really knows what's going on. It's her little way of keeping people from ever leaving, I suppose.

FRANK

Really?

ALICE

Somehow they think they've already left, or perhaps that they never arrived. She's very convincing in her way.

FRANK

Who *are* you? Why did you stop me from going through that door?

ALICE

Did I?

FRANK

You said "go." So I stopped.

ALICE

—

FRANK

Is it necessary that all this be so — enigmatic?

ALICE

Get out of this house.

FRANK

Gosh. Hospitality isn't much of a specialty with you. Is it?

ALICE

(A confrontation) I despise life's tourists, Mr. Travers.

FRANK

(Face to face) My situation is a little more complicated than that.

ALICE

It's never that complicated. We've all travelled our distances. And incidentally. When I said "go" I meant that you should keep going.

WILLY

(Entering) Hot milk! *(Stopping)* Oh. I forgot the milk. *(She goes off again)*

FRANK

(Following her off) Really, I don't want — thank you but...but I — I don't want you to make a fuss — you'll wake the other guests. *(A moment's pause)*

WALKER sneaks furtively down the stairs. Seeing ALICE, he descends a little further.

WALKER

Who are you? Do you work here?

ALICE

—

WALKER

(Quietly) Listen. This Mr. Travers. I take it he's in the room at the end of the hall.

ALICE

(Eye to eye) Why don't you go find out for yourself?

WALKER

(Confrontation) Why don't you show me?

WILLY

(Entering) Here we are.

FRANK

(Entering) Really, I do wish you'd keep your voice —
(Sees WALKER)

WILLY

Oh, dear.

WALKER

Good evening.

FRANK

Good evening.

WILLY

There's only the one glass.

WALKER

I didn't realize there was another guest.

FRANK

No. Staying long?

WALKER

Not any longer than I can help.

FRANK

Really? I was just passing through myself.

                    WALKER
Really?

                    FRANK
Really.

                    WILLY
How about a game of bid whist, everybody? *(Starts to organize a table, chairs and cards)*

                    WALKER
It's a bit late for cards, isn't it?

                    FRANK
Turning in?

                    WALKER
Thought I might. You?

                    FRANK
Not really tired.

                    WALKER
She seems determined for us to play.

                    FRANK
Logic isn't her strong suit.

                    WILLY
Mr. Travers will sit here. And Mr. — what should I call you, Mr. Travers?

                    FRANK
Yes. What should we call you?

                    WALKER
Anything will do.

                              WILLY
We don't have a fourth.

                             WALKER
That's a shame.

                              WILLY
There's Alice! *(Calling)* Alice! Bid-whist! *(Back to the men)*
Alice will play.

                              FRANK
Perfect.

                              ALICE
(Appearing) Has it occurred to you, Willy, that the two
guests might not *want* to stay the entire night.

                              FRANK
(Quickly sitting) I don't feel much like going anywhere.

                             WALKER
(Countering him) Neither do I.

                              WILLY
Mr. Travers and Travers are partners. Alice and I will
make up the winning team. Mr. Travers — you deal.

                             WALKER
If she's decided the winners, what's the point in playing?

                              FRANK
I don't think there is any.

                              ALICE
The point is to play anyway. It's terribly annoying.

                              FRANK
Who would like to cut the deck?

ALICE produces a meat cleaver.

FRANK

Never mind. *(He deals)*

WILLY

Alice!

WALKER

These are coasters.

WILLY

Yes. That's alright. You go ahead.

FRANK

(Out) It was the longest, most complicated card game of
my life.

WILLY

What's trump?

WALKER

The pictures of Prince Edward Island.

FRANK

Mr. Walker was even more agitated by the experience than
I was, which only led me to conclude that this was *not* part
of his plan.

WALKER

I think we lost again, Mr. Travers.

CLAYTON

(Appearing) Did you know then what you wanted to do?

FRANK

I told you. I didn't do anything. He did it.

CLAYTON

But you knew what would happen if he went through that
door.

FRANK

All I knew was that I was tired and I wanted to go to bed.

CLAYTON

Why didn't you?

FRANK

Where?

WILLY

What's the score now?

ALICE

Something.

WALKER

(Out) As the blind woman dealt the cards, I began to
really wonder what the plan was.

CLAYTON

Maybe there was no plan.

WALKER

(Out) And the game went on and on forever. Finally, the
loony one fell asleep so the blind one got up and
wandered off somewhere.

CLAYTON

Nobody around. Perfect opportunity.

WALKER

It was just me and him then.

                    FRANK
Just you and I.

                    WALKER
...he said.

                    CLAYTON
And what did you say?

                    WALKER
(To Frank) Yeah. Looks like it.

                    FRANK
So.

                    WALKER
So...

                    FRANK
So?

                    WALKER
So?

                    FRANK
So —

                    WALKER
So...?

                    FRANK
...so...

                    CLAYTON
Oh, for Christ's sake, how long did this go on for?

              FRANK & WALKER
Forever.

CLAYTON
How did you finally manage to get hold of his gun?

WALKER
Something fell.

A chandelier falls.

FRANK quickly drawing, closes his eyes and fires at the chandelier, dropping the gun immediately.

FRANK
Ah!

WILLY
(Waking) Whose bid?

WALKER
(Lunging towards FRANK) Agh!

They struggle with each other on the ground. WILLY watches. The lights fade on them momentarily as ALICE appears in another place, with CLAYTON.

ALICE
Yes. I heard a struggle. No. I didn't think it was unusual.

CLAYTON
Two men were killing each other.

ALICE
As I said...

CLAYTON
So I heard.

ALICE

Is there anything else I can help you with, Mr. Clayton.

CLAYTON

Just a couple of loose ends, Ma'am.

ALICE

Which I suppose you'd like to tie together somehow.

CLAYTON

Don't worry. I will.

ALICE

I'm not so optimistic as you, Mr. Clayton. I find life isn't as tidy as all that.

CLAYTON

(Looking around) Obviously.

ALICE

I suppose you're referring to the state of things around here.

CLAYTON

Well. It's a bit of a catastrophe. The authorities might have something to say about it. Before they shut it down.

ALICE

Talk to the proprietor, if you're going to talk to anyone.

CLAYTON

Oh. I will. Piece by piece I intend to take this place apart until I find exactly what I'm looking for. Whatever that is.

ALICE

I'm sure you'll find something, somewhere. Since you seem so intent on it.

CLAYTON

Yes, but so far, I'm not very satisfied with the answers I'm getting.

ALICE

So far, you haven't been given any, Mr. Clayton.

They disappear and in place of fighting we see FRANK tied to a chair. WALKER has the gun. WILLY sits, quietly watching the scene.

FRANK

What *is* this?

WALKER

Alright. Let's have it. The whole story.

FRANK

Story?

WALKER

Who are you with?

FRANK

Who are *you* with? With whom — are you — with...?

FRANK/WALKER

And — why — are — you — *following* — **me**?!

WALKER

(Out) Now this was something I didn't expect.

FRANK

What?

WALKER

You heard me.

FRANK
You're darn right I heard you! Are you insane?!

WALKER
Well, I am now.

FRANK
What kind of people are you working for?! Actually —
that should be — for what kind of people are you
working? And what do they want? Hhuh?

WALKER
This is some kind *psychology* you're working at here. What
are you trying to do to me?

FRANK
This is kidnapping, you know.

WALKER
So that's it. You want me to go to jail for the rest of my
rotten life.

FRANK
You're darn right I do.

WALKER
What have I ever done to you people?

FRANK
What people?

WALKER
You people? The organization you work for.

FRANK
The Free Advertiser Weekly?

WALKER
What are you talking about?

FRANK
What are *you* talking about?

A pause.

WALKER steps out of the scene.

WALKER
It took a bit of sorting out, but slowly the whole thing
started to unravel. At least, on the face of it. It was still
quite possible that one of us was lying. And I was positive
it wasn't me. *(Untying FRANK)* I didn't trust him of
course. But after listening to him for a while, I began to
realize he wasn't all that well-connected to the people in
charge. Just a nobody, really. In the scheme of things.

FRANK
Why would anyone follow *him?*

WALKER
Couldn't they send someone *important* after me? Did they
have to send *you?*

FRANK
The fact is, they couldn't be bothered to send *anyone.* Not
only is nobody *important* after you, Walker. Nobody's at *all*
is after you. There isn't so much as the *wind* at your back.

WALKER
Oh? Then perhaps you can explain all those secret
messages in the paper.

FRANK
One message.

                              WALKER
And the phony name?

                               FRANK
What about the wire strippers? If you want to arouse
suspicion, try an obscure piece of hardware.

                              WALKER
I was installing a dimmer switch. It's done all the time.
There's nothing "odd" about it. If you like to dim the
lights occasionally.

                               FRANK
Yes. In order to observe someone across the street.

                              WALKER
Alright. I was watching you. But only to find out why you
were watching me.

                               FRANK
But I wasn't watching you. Not until I realized that you —
were — watching — my God. Is it possible?

                              WALKER
What?

                               FRANK
That there's something...a little mistaken in our reading of
the situation here. That we've both jumped to the same
hasty conclusion?

                              WALKER
You'd like me to believe that, wouldn't you?

                               FRANK
What else is there to believe?

WALKER

If you haven't ruined my life, then who the hell *has?*

FRANK

(Out) I had no idea he'd suffered so much. According to the story that unfolded, he'd lived the life of a mongrel dog. Is it any wonder he thought someone else was responsible? How could you accept such a rotten existence as having been nothing more than an unlucky spin at the wheel?

WALKER & FRANK

I understand.

WALKER

...he said. But how could he? *(To FRANK)* How could you?

FRANK

Wait a minute. You say you were struck by lightning when you were three? I wasn't struck, and I wasn't three. I was six. But it came very close. I've never told anybody this, Walker. Lightning hit our garage roof.

WALKER

Hardly the same.

FRANK

(A little to himself) Yes, but it was from that day onward that I felt compelled to avoid things. That danger was somewhere close at hand. It *changed* me. Formed me into the maladjusted and neurotic person I am today. But here's the other thing, and I find this sort of — well, remarkable. It was forked lightning, Walker. Was yours forked lightning?

WALKER

I don't remember. I was three for God's sake.

FRANK

But think about it. There could be a connection here.
Somehow. The two of us. Connected by a — an — event.
Perhaps even struck by the very same bolt of lightning.
Don't you sense the sad beauty of it? The destiny that
shaped our lives and brought us together?

WALKER

Are you suggesting, even for a minute, you've put up with
the same shit in life that I have? Believe me. There's no
connection between us. Poetical or otherwise.

FRANK

No. I've haven't suffered as much as you, but I've suffered
as long. The point is, we've both suffered. And yet, we like
to think of ourselves as having been singled out for some
kind of special, horrible treatment. You know — when I
hear the whole, pathetic story, I'm compelled to think of
you as an insect, Walker. An average, not very special
spider, let's say. A frightened spider, really, frozen on the
wall, trying desperately to pretend it's not there, as the
newspaper is slowly folded, and it, thinking, "Why are
they going after *me?*" There's no reason. Except perhaps
that it's vaguely annoying. And a little ugly. Nothing
more. I'm afraid nobody cares about you Walker. And
nobody cares about me.

WALKER

That simply can't be true.

FRANK

Yes, but like most things that simply can't be true — it
probably is.

They both fall despondent, and silent for a moment.

FRANK

I'm sorry, Walker. I wish life could have been more sinister.

WILLY

(*Suddenly, after a long pause, lightning*) Oh. I forgot I was here. (*Pause*) Well, would you care for anything now that I am? (*Pause*) I don't mind, Mr. Travers. I like to be of some use around here, since nobody else is. It's been like this for as long as I can remember. I arrived here, once, just like everybody else. There wasn't so much as a bellman to collect my things. I went to my room and just sat on my bed. For days. Alice would drift by in a dream, now and again, and disappear. "What a strange way she has of running things" I thought. Not a towel or a tea biscuit to be had. Days passed into weeks and I began to really wonder. I had to make my own breakfast, my own bed. One day, passing by Alice's room, and noticing she wasn't anywhere about, I snuck in and peeked around. But — no sooner had I entered when she came charging up from behind me. "Well!" she said, "It's about time you made up the room. The service in this place is terrible!!" She thought I was the management, you see, and I found myself surrendering to her conviction. Over time. But don't tell Alice. She'd be very upset. You know how she is with guests. And she'd hardly be pleased to discover I was one. After all this time. Who wants to know that there's no one in charge of things? It leaves us with nobody to complain about. When things go wrong. As they so often do. But one does wonder when on earth they're going to finally show up, these absentee proprietors. I'm staying only as long as that. To pay my bill. And I'll be on my way once again. In the meantime, you must forgive poor Alice. She doesn't see things the way you and I do. As a matter of fact, she doesn't see them at all. So quite naturally she assumes that you're evil. People are always much worse when you imagine them.

FRANK

It's true, Walker. She has a point. I only *think* you're bad.
Who knows? Maybe you're not. What makes you all that
different from *me?*

WALKER

—

FRANK

There's too little faith in this world, Walker.

WILLY

Shall I get some? *(She goes)*

FRANK

(Calling after her) Faith. I said "faith." Never mind.
(Offering his hand) Here. Take my hand, Walker.

WALKER

It's unbelievable. I feel so — I'm such an impulsive person
by nature. I just assumed — you seemed so —

FRANK

Naturally, you did.

WALKER

I'm sorry. It's the strain of being alone in the world that
does it. Do you suppose I could — hug you? Would that
be too much?

FRANK

Yes. But —

They hug.

WALKER

(Turning to the audience in the hug) What's the bastard up to now?

FRANK

Yes, well...

Ending the embrace, they separate, a little embarrassed by their affection.

WALKER

That feels...better. Doesn't it?

FRANK

Doesn't it.

WALKER

(Turning away) Conniving son of a bitch.

FRANK

(Out) The poor jerk. Quite naturally he was distraught. Terribly distraught as a matter of fact. Have I mentioned the word "suicide"?

CLAYTON

(Appearing) Several times. Is that the story you're going with?

FRANK

You don't believe me.

CLAYTON

You followed a man to a hotel. You registered under another name. You had a gun.

FRANK

Excuse me. *He* had the gun.

CLAYTON

But I thought you came to an understanding?

FRANK

In theory, yes. But you never really lose your faith in skepticism. People are people, Clayton — after all. They have minds. And God only knows what's in them.

CLAYTON

So you lead him to his death. Is that what you're saying?

FRANK

As a matter of fact, Clayton, I was doing my best to stop him.

WALKER

So what's in the room at the end of the hall?

FRANK

I think you'll find there's nothing there.

WALKER

Listen. It's not that I don't trust you or anything. Because I do.

FRANK

You should.

WALKER

Yes, but it's nice to have the evidence. Proof that you're a nobody. And nothing in that room up there to prove otherwise.

FRANK

Nothing at all.

WALKER

So *you* go.

FRANK

Why?

WALKER

I've got the gun.

FRANK

It's a little difficult to prove to you there's nothing there, if *I* go. I already know what isn't there. You're the skeptic.

WALKER

(Out) I knew he was bluffing.

FRANK

(Out) I knew he knew I was bluffing.

WALKER

Speaking as a friend, I want to believe you, but how can I, Frank?

FRANK

Well, friendship is a complicated thing. It usually means having faith in someone you probably shouldn't.

WALKER

I can't figure out if you want me to go up there...or if you don't. See?

FRANK

I'll be honest with you. I don't.

WALKER

You don't. That means you do. But maybe you're smarter than that, which means you really don't. Which means I *should*. Right?

FRANK

Then maybe you should.

                         WALKER
Which means I *shouldn't*. Which means I should, which
means I shouldn't.

                         CLAYTON
·   Oh for God's sake!

                         WALKER
Which means I *will*.

                         FRANK
Whatever.

                         WALKER
Whatever.

A tense pause. Suddenly, FRANK runs at WALKER.
WALKER shoots, and FRANK slumps back into his chair,
dead, eyes wide open. The gunshot brings WILLY.

                         WALKER
He ran at me. It was self-defence.

                         CLAYTON
Any witnesses?

                         WILLY
Did somebody call?!

                         CLAYTON
Credible witnesses?

                         WALKER
It was *self-defence*.

                         CLAYTON
He wasn't armed, Walker. You don't have much of a case.

WALKER

How's this for a case? He ruined my life.

CLAYTON

Sure. So you set out to murder him. I understand. And
then you stuck around to cover up the evidence.

WALKER

(Looking upstairs) I was *looking* for evidence, Clayton.

CLAYTON

Of what?

WALKER

Anything!

WILLY

Turning in?

WALKER

(To WILLY) Yeah. I think I'll turn in now. Mr. Travers is
going to stay up for a while. Aren't you Mr. Travers?

Holding FRANK's head from behind, he makes him nod.

"Yes, I am." Alright then. I'll be turning in. Goodnight.

WALKER goes up the stairs as WILLY watches him.

WILLY

Goodnight, Mr. Travers. *(A pause, then turning to FRANK)*
Away he goes, then.

WALKER

(From off) Ahhhhhhhh!

FRANK

(Suddenly coming alive) And away he went. Fortunately, I must have fainted.

CLAYTON

And how bad a shot was he, Frank?

FRANK

Obviously bad enough.

CLAYTON

Must have been. We never even found a bullet.

WILLY

Nightcap, Mr. Travers?

FRANK

Not for me, thanks. I've got to run.

WILLY

Oh. I'll see if we have any of that.

CLAYTON

But we found the gun.

FRANK

Is there a problem? You found the gun. That's good, isn't it?

CLAYTON

Not so good for you. The gun is a fake. A prop.

FRANK

Prop? I didn't know that. I thought I was in danger. I *was* in danger.

CLAYTON

Were in danger, yes. But not anymore.

FRANK

I didn't know.

CLAYTON

So you left. Generally the person who leaves the scene of a crime is the one guilty of it.

FRANK

I was the one who'd been *murdered*, Clayton.

CLAYTON

Let's be a little more precise than that. *Not* murdered, is a little more precise.

FRANK

Call it what you want. I felt I had to get out of there.

CLAYTON

Of course you did.

Transition out of house.

FRANK

Make my way back into my own life somehow.

MONA appears, now a fabulous star.

MONA

What life? I thought you didn't have a life.

FRANK

Well, I don't.

MONA

How did you find me, anyways?

FRANK

I searched you out. It wasn't difficult, Mona. You're everywhere.

MONA

Do you know how many people have come out of my past, Frank? Just because I've done a couple of movies now? People who don't have a life and are looking for one? This is like — I can't handle this. Look at me. This has all happened so fast I haven't even had time to fire my agent yet.

FRANK

You know a lot of people.

MONA

Yeah. But they're all the *wrong* people.

FRANK

Somebody who could help me get started again. Please.

MONA

You told me once to be ruthless, Frank.

FRANK

I did?

MONA

(*To someone else*) I'm not wearing that!

FRANK

So I did.

MONA disappears.

It was her fault that I was alive. She gave me a fake gun. I would have been dead otherwise. That would have solved a lot of my problems.

LAWRENCE appears suddenly, in the truck.

LAWRENCE
Not really, Frank. Because then you'da had to reckon up with the Lord before you were ready. Now you're on the right side of the road, making your way to salvation. Alleluia, and amen. Just don't cross over that line, brother. Or you'll be headed right back the other way.

FRANK
Do you really think religion is the answer, Lawrence?

LAWRENCE
Something's gotta keep us on this road, man.

LAWRENCE disappears.

FRANK
They don't understand. Who does? Walker did. He understood. Your enemies always understand you. It's your friends you have to watch out for.

ASTRID
(Appearing) What friends?

FRANK
I thought maybe I'd go to a counsellor. I don't even know why. Guidance? I mean — where am I going? I've got a ticket here to some unknown event that's already taken place. Is that my future? There's a letter "B" and a number "4" somewhere. Okay. I know that much. But how can you look *before* you in life, if you don't know what's there? I feel like I'm driving a road, looking in the rear view mirror. Guessing where I'm going by where I've gone, and arriving only by the grace of some benign accident.

ASTRID

So. Do you want to get back together, then?

FRANK

Not really. Do you?

ASTRID

No. Not really. *(She drifts away)*

FRANK

That whole situation with Walker gave me such focus in my life. There he was. Making me crazy. What's making me crazy now? Who knows?

MILLIE

(Appearing) Who knows anything?

FRANK

Astrid?

CLAYTON

(Following MILLIE) Well, I'm sure you can come up with something.

FRANK

(Going off) Astrid?

CLAYTON

(With photos) Recognize either of these men?

MILLIE

Not only do I don't recognized them — I wished I didn't.

CLAYTON

We all wish we didn't know criminals.

MILLIE

Criminals?

CLAYTON
What else can you tell me?

MILLIE
I have no information.

CLAYTON
You're a psychic.

MILLIE
I knew that you would say that. But what does it mean?

CLAYTON
You tell *me*.

MILLIE
People come to me for help. I tell them what I see.

CLAYTON
And what did you see?

MILLIE
Two men, running from one another, who collide.

CLAYTON
That's very profound. It's no wonder you charge good money for that.

MILLIE
Of course. I report the extrasensory.

CLAYTON
But not the extra income. From what I understand.

MILLIE
(*Short pause*) What answers would you like?

CLAYTON
What answers have you got?

MILLIE
You must follow the stors, Mr. Clayton.

CLAYTON
Stores?

MILLIE
The mystic stors. Stap by stap. To reach the answer.

CLAYTON
Reach the...? Step by...? *Stairs!* You mean *stairs.*

MILLIE
Look up and you will see. Your destiny is there.

MILLIE leaves and CLAYTON follows.

CLAYTON
Ma'am?

WALKER
(Coming down the stairs) And what happened to his body?
It can't have just disappeared. The last time I saw him he
was dead in a chair. Obviously they moved in very
quickly to dispose of it. I wasn't about to stick around and
find out.

ALICE
(Appearing) Leaving? So soon.

WALKER
I've got to get away from here.

ALICE

Good.

WALKER

You ought to have warned me about that room.
Fortunately, there was no knob on the door. I couldn't get
in. But I could tell something was wrong by the wiring.
There was a short in the light switch when I turned it on.
That was the first thing that struck me. Or should I say —
gave me a small electrical shock. "Bingo," I thought. Then,
when I peeked through a hole in the door, where the knob
had been, I couldn't help but notice it was raining inside.
That was a pretty good indication.

ALICE

This house is falling away piece by piece. Little bit by little
bit, the edge of the world comes nearer.

WALKER

Are you with them?

ALICE

I'm not with anybody.

WALKER

To tell you the truth, I don't trust blind people. I always
feel like they're looking at something I can't see.

ALICE

Just infinity, Mr. Travers.

WILLY enters with an empty tray.

WILLY

Breakfast!

ALICE

Never mind, Willy. He's not staying. None of them is staying. They can't abide the service here.

WALKER

By the way — what have you done with the body?

ALICE

Body? Willy. Have you seen a body?

WILLY

Really?

ALICE

We appear to be missing one.

WILLY

No. Have you?

WALKER

Never mind. Someone's already taken care of it I see. *(Moving away)* But who? I left Blind Alice and her friend Willy where I found them, and went back in the direction I'd come. I discovered myself headed back to the town where I'd first seen him. And what do you think I saw? Him. Same bus stop.

WALKER and FRANK spot each other and freeze.

FRANK

Same situation. I couldn't believe it. As if the whole thing had never happened in the first place.

FINN

(Appearing) You're not going to go running off again this time, are you? Leave me here with nobody to be in charge of.

FRANK

That's a preposition, Mr. Finn.

FINN

Well...a job offer, anyway.

FRANK

I thought you were retiring.

FINN

Work is so much easier.

FRANK

Well...that's very considerate of you, Mr. Finn, and I'll
think about it, but I have some other business to take care
of first. A criminal action.

FINN

(*Leaving*) Oh. You oughtn't to tell me, Frank. I just don't
want to know.

FRANK

I'm *filing* a criminal action, not committing one. He tried to
kill me, and I have witnesses. I'm going to charge Mr.
Walker with attempted murder.

Transition.

CLAYTON

I'm afraid he's already filed a charge against *you*.

FRANK

What?

CLAYTON

Attempted murder.

133

FRANK

He can't do that.

CLAYTON

You're right. He can't. Neither can you. The police will decide who can charge who with what, for what, where, when, with what witnesses, whenever, wherever, and with whose authority.

FRANK

But he attempted to murder *me*.

CLAYTON

So you'll both be charged and you'll both serve time.

FRANK

Time? Serve *time?*

WALKER

(Appearing) This is just exactly what he wanted to accomplish. Finish me off in jail. One way or the other.

FRANK & WALKER

"I'll take him down with me."

FRANK

...I thought. And God help me, I did. Actually — we sort of took each other down. There wasn't a lot of evidence...

WALKER

...except what we said about each other.

FRANK

As well, the witnesses were not as forthcoming as I thought they'd be. And those that were, well...

WILLY

(Appearing, as if on the witness stand) Oh. I certainly was.

FRANK

They each had their own unique version of events.

ALICE

(Appearing as witness) I didn't see a thing.

WALKER

Everybody always does.

JACK

(Appearing) It was this big. No. This big. No...

FRANK

People will contradict each other with absolute abandon when they get a chance. It seems to be the outcome of asking anyone an opinion. The truth is just a bunch of little lies in the right order. It's why I like order. In a way I don't mind going to jail. It gives me time to think about the proper arrangement of things. It's only a short sentence, anyway. The attempted murder, as it happens, was thrown out on a number of grounds, and in favor of the lesser charge of public mischief. For both of us, of course. In sentencing, the judge, a person who (apparently) I rudely delivered an *Advertiser Weekly* to once, said that in deference to my gardening background, he could understand how two weeds might get tangled up in one another...

WALKER

Or how two wires could get crossed.

WALKER & FRANK

But not two grown men.

Sound of a gavel.

135

FRANK

Well, perhaps he doesn't quite understand human nature as Walker and I have come to. As it turns out, people are a little like — slugs, really. One just can't imagine why on earth they would exist, except, perhaps, to keep each other company. (And of course to leave a trail of slime.) In sentencing, the judge suggested that such enmity as ours should always be brought face to face with itself. So he condemned us to that world for a time. Not only were we sent to the same prison; we were made to share the same prison cell.

WALKER, with a bloody nose, is sitting in prison, across from FRANK.

WALKER

Come to think of it, maybe that blind woman was never really blind at all?

FRANK

(Reading a paper) Keep your head up. It'll stop the bleeding.

WALKER

That's a — smart way to spy on people. Don't you think? Or you could pretend you were deaf, and they'd talk about you and you'd know what they were saying. But you wouldn't let on. *(Pause)* Or you could pretend you were reading a newspaper, when really you were planning something.

FRANK

Trust me. I'm not planning anything.

WALKER

Oh. Well, then I won't worry about it.

FRANK
(With newspaper) Look at this. Some guy just won a big lottery.

WALKER
Some guy always *does.*

FRANK
With the same name as yours. Henry Walker.

WALKER
(Grabbing the paper) Let me see that. *(He reads)* That's me. I gave him my...

WALKER quietly begins crying.

FRANK
How's that for luck?

FRANK watches him, as the lights slowly fade.

CLAYTON
(In another place) We couldn't get a conviction in the end. Not a real one.

ALICE
(Knitting) I told you what I saw. They're in jail now. What more do you want?

CLAYTON
The truth.

ALICE
The truth has a way of coming apart in your hands, Mr. Clayton. Keep pulling at the thread and you'll unravel the whole cloth.

CLAYTON

There are just too many questions unresolved for me in this case. Now that I have the perpetrators, I intend to uncover the crime. Something's going on somewhere. Always has been. Always will. I won't be fooled into thinking otherwise. I'll have to take you in for questioning.

ALICE

I belong here, Mr. Clayton. One ought to stay where one belongs. Don't you think? Be satisfied enough with the way things are.

CLAYTON

(*Retrieving knob in door where FRANK left it*) I'm never satisfied that I've reached the end of a case until I've actually reached it. And even then, I'm never sure that I've ever actually reached it. Ever. When I was a child, I remember I saw a terrific lightning storm in the distance once. But while others stupidly sat in their windowsills and watched evil flash it's electric teeth at the world, I went off in search of it. From horizon to horizon. Never witness to the event. Always arriving afterwards, like some breathless academic. Just one step behind history. Shovel in hand. I'll wait for those men. And when they're free again, I'll follow them. Forever, if I have to.

ALICE

Your life has a kind of theme to it. That's comforting.

CLAYTON

For now, I'd like to know where these stairs *really* lead.

ALICE

Of course you would.

CLAYTON

We have a psychic working with us on the case now. She
said we might find some answers up here. We must follow
the stairs, she said. What do you say?

ALICE

You'll find nothing.

CLAYTON

(*Mounting the stairs*) Of course, you've *told* me there's
nothing. But who ever believes what people tell them? Do
we ever *really* know until we see it for ourselves? Even
when we look at something, we wonder — is it actually
there? And does it constitute hard evidence, or has it been
manufactured, in order to *look* like evidence? That's what
keeps us wondering. Looking. Digging. Searching.
Penetrating. That's what keeps us going. (*He disappears*)

WILLY, with some idea about tea, enters with a tray.

WILLY

Oh. (*Looking about*) They all went off somewhere. All the
gentlemen. Off they went.

ALICE

(*Knitting*) Yes. (*She pauses for a moment to listen to a man
falling*) Off they go, Willy. Some this way, some that. Each
to their own end.

A moment of attentive silence.

ALICE

What's that sound?

WILLY

Perhaps it's just things coming to their conclusion.

ALICE
Is someone coming up the road?

WILLY
(Looking off) One can only hope.

In another light, WALKER plays Bingo, as FRANK calls the numbers.

FRANK
Under the "I," seventeen... "O" sixty-four... "N" thirty-three.... *(Producing a ticket stub from his pocket)* ..."B" four....

WALKER
(Looking out) Bingo!

Fade. A waltz plays out.

The End